HAL LEONARD KEYBOARD STYLE SERIES

COUNTRY PIANO

THE COMPLETE GUIDE WITH AUDIO!

To access audio visit:
www.halleonard.com/mylibrary

4068-2796-8999-2135

BY MARK HARRISON

ISBN 978-0-634-06709-9

HAL•LEONARD®
CORPORATION
7777 W. BLUEMOUND RD. P.O. BOX 13819 MILWAUKEE, WI 53213

In Australia Contact:
Hal Leonard Australia Pty. Ltd.
4 Lentara Court
Cheltenham, Victoria, 3192 Australia
Email: ausadmin@halleonard.com

T0033981

Visit Hal Leonard Online at www.halleonard.com

INTRODUCTION

Welcome to *Country Piano*. If you've ever wanted to play country music on the piano but weren't quite sure how, then you've come to the right place! Whatever your playing level, this book/audio package will help you sound more authentic in your country piano stylings.

After reviewing some essential chords and scales, we'll dig into the voicing techniques and rhythmic patterns that are vital for the country pianist. We'll focus on "comping" (or accompaniment) patterns as well as "solo" passages and fills—all of which will help you to create your own piano parts on a variety of country tunes and progressions! We'll also take a tour through the different stages of country music's evolution, from the early days of cowboy music and bluegrass, through honky-tonk and the Nashville sound, and then on to contemporary country and country rock. We'll spotlight the important country pianists in these styles and see how to incorporate their vocabulary into our own music.

Several tunes in different country styles are included in the "Style File" chapter at the end of the book. Jam with the rhythm section on these tunes using the play-along tracks—this is a great way to develop your country piano chops and apply them within different styles.

Good luck with it!

—*Mark Harrison*

About the Audio

On the accompanying audio, you'll find demonstrations of the piano parts in this book. Solo examples feature the left-hand part on the left channel and the right-hand part on the right channel to facilitate easy "hands separate" practice. Some recordings—like those in the "Style File" chapter—include a rhythm section as well as piano. For these tunes, the rhythm section is on the left channel, and the piano on the right channel. To play along with the rhythm section only, simply turn down the right channel.

About the Author

Mark Harrison is a *Keyboard Magazine* columnist and an educational author whose books are used by thousands of musicians worldwide. His TV credits include *Saturday Night Live, American Justice, Celebrity Profiles,* and many other shows and commercials. As a working keyboardist in the Los Angeles area, Mark performs regularly with the top-flight Steely Dan tribute band Doctor Wu, as well as the critically-acclaimed Mark Harrison Quintet. He has also shared the stage with top musicians such as John Molo (Bruce Hornsby band) and Jimmy Haslip (Yellowjackets), and is currently co-writing an R&B/pop project with the Grammy-winning songwriter Ron Dunbar.

Other instructional books by Mark Harrison include *Contemporary Music Theory* (Levels 1–3) and *The Pop Piano Book*, also published by Hal Leonard Corporation. For further information on the author's musical activities and educational products, please visit *www.harrisonmusic.com.*

CONTENTS

Chapter 1
WHAT IS COUNTRY MUSIC?

Country is an American music style that emerged in the 1920s. Although it has continued to evolve and develop right up through the present day, there are certain characteristics that have been more-or-less consistent throughout its development. For example, the lyrics of country music are typically "true-to-life," dealing with subjects such as home and family, relationship issues, working-man problems, drinking, etc. The vocals are often stark and emotional and project a storytelling quality (especially in the more traditional styles). Musically, instruments such as fiddle, steel guitar, and mandolin are signature sounds, typically paired with basic chord progressions (e.g., I–IV–V) and simple song forms.

The evolution of country music has been somewhat cyclical in nature, with periods when the style has incorporated elements from other genres (in response to demographic shifts or to reach a wider audience), followed by periods when the style has returned to its more traditional roots. Along the way, country has blended with gospel, blues, pop, and rock music, creating hybrid styles such as country blues, country rock, and so on. In a similar fashion to the development of jazz, the traditional country styles have not disappeared at all, but retain their following alongside the more modern and hybrid styles. The following are considered the main eras and subgenres within country music:

Old-Time Country

One of country's most important ancestors was "old time" or "fiddle" music from the Appalachian mountains. This was a sparse style that developed in the late 1800s, with the vocal being accompanied by fiddle and/or banjo. In the mid 1920s, with a further blending of folk, minstrel, vaudeville and gospel influences, country music officially arrived. The first important recording stars were Jimmie Rodgers and the Carter Family, on the Victor Records label. In the mid 1920s, The Grand Ole Opry in Nashville, Tennessee became established as the premier country performance venue, and the top names in country music continued to play at the Opry throughout the twentieth century.

Although many early country artists thought little of using the piano in their lineups, pianists can nonetheless be heard on some recordings from this early period. Lillian Armstrong played the piano on some of Jimmie Rodgers's sessions, and country icon Roy Acuff (a famous performer at the Opry) had pianist Jimmie Riddle in his band.

Cowboy Music

This style is credited with putting the "western" into country 'n' western music. A lot of the songs in this style were made popular through the cowboy films of the 1930s and '40s, featuring artists such as Roy Rogers and Gene Autry. Rogers was also a member of the Sons of the Pioneers, who were the foremost vocal and instrumental group during this period. (This group continued to perform with various lineups up until the 1990s and was very popular.) The cowboy style is rhythmically and harmonically simple, with a focus on the emotion and story conveyed in the lyrics.

Western Swing

This style evolved in Texas and Oklahoma in the 1930s and '40s, featuring string bands with a fiddle lead. Elements of jazz, big band, blues, and Dixieland were blended to create the Western swing sound, and new instruments such as drums and Hawaiian steel guitar were also introduced. This was first and foremost dance music, fusing the culture of the Southwest with jazz and swing sounds. Important artists in this style include Bob Wills (known as the "king of Western swing"), Cliff Bruner, and Milton Brown. Wills and Brown were also members of the Light Crust Doughboys, a famous group from this period.

The piano played an important role in the development of this style. Fred "Papa" Calhoun is credited with being the first pianist in Western swing, having joined Milton Brown and his Musical Brownies in 1932. Other pianists in this style included Al Stricklin (Bob Wills's Texas Playboys), Moon Mullican (who worked with Cliff Bruner), and John "Smokey" Wood.

Bluegrass

This style has a very distinct up-tempo sound driven by the banjo and mandolin, often with a busy ar-peggiated accompaniment. Bluegrass was pioneered in the 1940s by the singer and mandolin player Bill Monroe, together with Earl Scruggs and Lester Flatt. Scruggs's driving "three-finger" banjo technique became a signature sound and helped popularize the style. In the late 1940s, Scruggs and Flatt left Monroe's band to form the Foggy Mountain Boys, who continued to record for Columbia throughout the '50s and '60s.

Bluegrass music is not noted for its pianists, although Bill Monroe's touring band did feature Sally Ann Forrester on accordion. However, we can certainly have fun in adapting these great banjo and mandolin patterns to the piano!

Honky-Tonk

This was a city-inspired style, with lyrical themes of celebration and sin, named after the "honky-tonks" or taverns of the 1930s and '40s. The singing style owed much to Jimmie Rodgers, and the instrumentation included the drums and steel guitar popularized in Western swing. Honky-tonk (and in particular the lyrical themes it uses) remains a major influence on subsequent country styles to this day. Major artists from this period include Hank Williams, Ernest Tubb, and Lefty Frizell.

Noted pianists in this style include Fred Rose (Hank Williams), Owen Bradley (Ernest Tubb), and the session ace Hargus "Pig" Robbins.

The Nashville Sound

In the late 1950s and early '60s the Nashville sound emerged. This was a produced, formula-driven blend of pop and country, created to reach a wider audience. Although it still had some of the storytelling quality of honky-tonk, musically it was very smooth, eschewing fiddle and steel guitar in favor of lush strings and vocal arrangements. Famous Nashville-era artists include Jim Reeves, Patsy Cline, Eddy Arnold, and Tammy Wynette.

Probably the most noted pianist from this period is Floyd Cramer, whose distinctive "slip-note" style was featured on many Nashville sessions. Cramer's style continues to influence contemporary artists as diverse as rock pianist Bruce Hornsby and jazz pianist David Benoit. Other noted pianists and session musicians from this period include Marvin Hughes, and the aforementioned Owen Bradley and Hargus "Pig" Robbins.

Outlaw

The late 1960s and '70s saw the emergence of a more traditional country sound known as "outlaw." This harder-edged style was a reaction to the smooth, formula-driven Nashville sound. The term "outlaw" started as a nickname for the lifestyles of some of the artists of the period and was then used as a description of this particular country style. Although outlaw music signaled a return to the roots of country, the style nonetheless had considerable success in "crossing over" to the rock market of the time. Noted outlaw artists include Willie Nelson, Waylon Jennings, Johnny Cash, and Merle Haggard.

Noted pianists in this style (aside from the aforementioned Owen Bradley and Hargus Robbins) include Barry Beckett (Willie Nelson), Merrill Moore and Larry Butler (Johnny Cash), and Billy Liebert (Merle Haggard).

Country Rock

This style was born on the West Coast in the late 1960s and '70s, and blended country melodies and harmonies with rock rhythms and instrumentation. Of course, country music was integral to the birth of rock 'n' roll, and the influence of country on rock artists is felt all the way from Elvis Presley through to Sting and Beck. The term "country rock" however, is normally used to describe artists such as the Byrds (after Gram Parsons joined the band), the Eagles, and Poco, who are associated with this particular era.

Noted pianists/keyboardists from this period include Glenn Frey (the Eagles), Earl Ball (the Byrds), and session ace Larry Knechtel (the Byrds and Poco, among others).

Urban Cowboy

The "urban cowboy" movement emerged in the early 1980s and led country music away from its roots towards an easy-listening pop format (much to the chagrin of some country traditionalists). It was designed to appeal to a more urban audience, and signaled a further blurring of the lines between country and pop. Famous urban cowboy-period artists include John Conlee, Alabama, and Reba McEntire.

Noted pianists/keyboardists from this period include the aforementioned Hargus Robbins (Reba McEntire and many others), David Briggs, and session ace Barry Beckett (Alabama and many others).

New Country

The term "new country" is used here to describe a blend of "new traditionalist" and "pop crossover" styles. Beginning in the mid 1980s, a new generation of stars reconnected country music to younger audiences, in a way that was closer to the style's roots and yet had crossover appeal. This was typically done by blending traditional country elements (such the vocal style, steel guitar, and violin) within a radio-friendly rock framework. This recipe proved extraordinarily successful for Garth Brooks in the 1990s, who became the biggest-selling country artist of all time. Other important new country/new traditionalist artists include George Strait, Ricky Skaggs, Randy Travis, the Judds, and Alan Jackson.

Important pianists/keyboardists in contemporary country include the session aces Matt Rollins (Randy Travis and many others) and John Hobbs (Shania Twain and many others), as well as the above-mentioned Barry Beckett. Also the pianist Bruce Hornsby, while not a country artist per se, created a unique piano-based blend of country, pop, and rock in the 1980s, before absorbing more R&B and jazz influences in the '90s.

Now let's see how chords and scales are used in country music (in Chapter 2), before focusing on country progressions and piano techniques (starting in Chapter 3). On with the show!

Chapter 2
SCALES and CHORDS

Major scales and keys

First of all, we'll take a look at the **major scale**, which is the fundamental basis of harmony in most contemporary music styles. I recommend that you think of this scale in terms of the intervals it contains—whole step, whole step, half step, whole step, whole step, whole step and half step—as this most closely parallels how the ear relates to the scale. Here is the C major scale, showing these intervals:

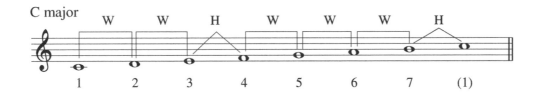

This major scale pattern (W-W-H-W-W-W-H) can be applied to any root note. Here for your reference are all of the major scales. After C major, the next seven scales contain flats, i.e., F major has one flat, B♭ major has two flats, and so on. The next seven scales contain sharps, i.e., G major has one sharp, D major has two sharps, and so on.

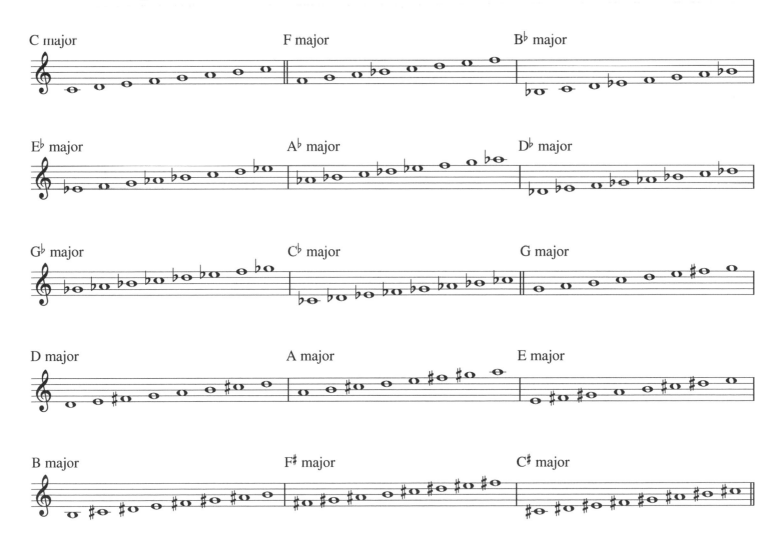

7

In this book, we'll work with music examples in various keys. For example, a tune will be "in the key of C" if the note C is heard as the tonic or "home base," and if the notes used are within the C major scale (except for any additional sharped or flatted notes occurring in the music).

A key signature is a group of flats or sharps at the beginning of the music that lets you know which key you are in. Here for your reference are all of the major key signatures:

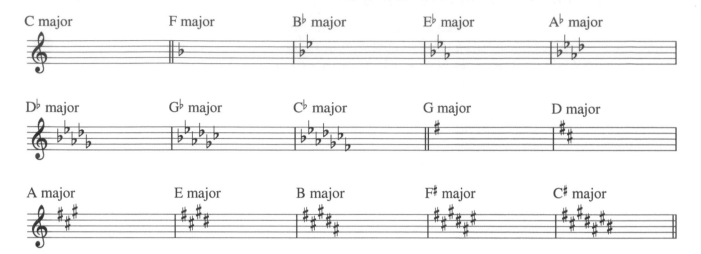

The Mixolydian mode

A **mode** or modal scale is created when we take a major scale and displace it to start on another scale degree. An example of this is the Mixolydian mode, created when the major scale is displaced to start on the 5th degree, as in the following example of a C major scale displaced to create the G Mixolydian mode:

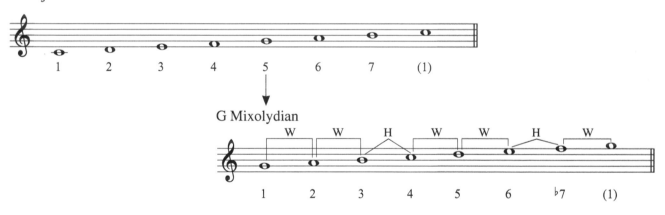

If you compare the two scales above, you'll see that the notes are the same; they just begin and end at different points—C major begins and ends on C, G Mixolydian begins and ends on G. So what's the difference? Each scale has a different implied tonic or root, and therefore a different pattern of whole and half steps (from one note to the next), resulting in a different overall sound.

A somewhat quicker way to derive the Mixolydian mode is to build it from its own root, following the above step pattern. When seen this way, the Mixolydian mode basically a major scale with a flatted 7th (1-2-3-4-5-6-♭7). For example, here's the Mixolydian mode built from the root C.

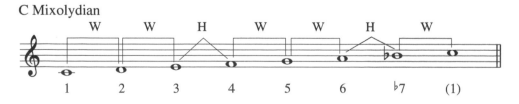

The Mixolydian mode is the basic scale source for a dominant seventh chord (more about those shortly) and will therefore be very useful in styles such as country blues, which are built around dominant chords.

The pentatonic scale

The **pentatonic scale** (a.k.a. the major pentatonic scale) is a five-note scale widely used in country music, as well as in rock, blues, and jazz. It can be derived by taking the major scale and removing the 4th and 7th degrees:

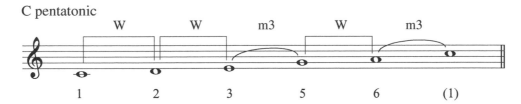

Note that from bottom to top, this scale now contains the following intervals: whole step, whole step, minor 3rd, whole step, and minor 3rd. Again, the interval pattern is what gives the scale its unique sound. This scale is extremely useful for creating fills and soloing, as we'll see later.

Triads and seventh chords

TRIADS

There are four main types of triad (three-part chord) in common usage: **major**, **minor**, **augmented**, and **diminished**. The following example shows each of these triads in treble and bass clefs, built from the root of C:

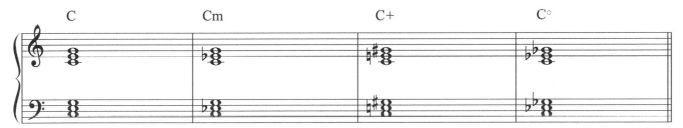

Note that these triads are formed by building the following intervals above the root note:

Major triad:	Major 3rd and perfect 5th (1–3–5)
Minor triad:	Minor 3rd and perfect 5th (1–♭3–5)
Augmented triad:	Major 3rd and augmented 5th (1–3–♯5)
Diminished triad:	Minor 3rd and diminished 5th (1–♭3–♭5)

If we construct triads from each degree of the major scale, and stay within the restrictions of the scale, we create **diatonic** triads. The following example shows the diatonic triads found within the C major scale:

Relating the above triads to the four main triad types, note that **major** triads are built from the 1st, 4th, and 5th major scale degrees, **minor** triads are built from the 2nd, 3rd, and 6th scale degrees, and a **diminished** triad is built from the 7th scale degree. (The augmented triad does not occur anywhere in the diatonic series.)

major	minor	minor	major	major	minor	diminished
I	ii	iii	IV	V	vi	vii°

Knowledge of the diatonic triads is important to the country musician, as many country songs use diatonic triad progressions—particularly, the **I, IV**, and **V** chords (i.e., the major triads built from the 1st, 4th and 5th degrees of the key). You should strive to learn the "one, four, and five" chords in as many major keys as possible!

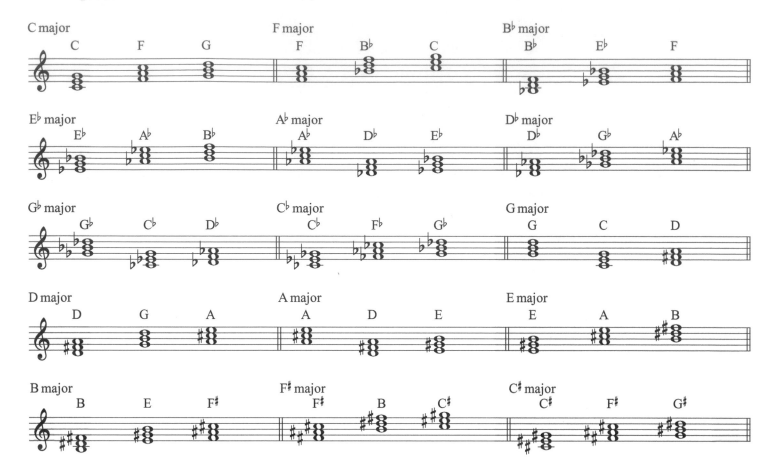

SEVENTH AND SIXTH CHORDS

The four-part chords most commonly used in country music are the **major seventh**, **minor seventh**, **minor sixth**, and **dominant seventh** chords. The following example shows these four-part chords in treble and bass clefs, built from the root of C:

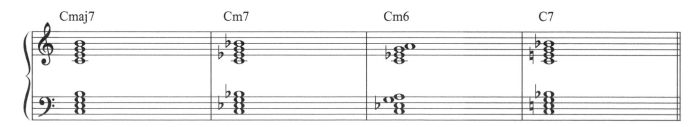

Note that these chords are formed by building the following intervals above the root note:

Major seventh chord:	Major 3rd, perfect 5th, and major 7th (1-3-5-7)
Minor seventh chord:	Minor 3rd, perfect 5th, and minor 7th (1-♭3-5-♭7)
Minor sixth chord:	Minor 3rd, perfect 5th, and major 6th (1-♭3-5-6)
Dominant seventh chord:	Major 3rd, perfect 5th, and minor 7th (1-3-5-♭7)

Again, if we construct seventh chords from each degree of the major scale, and stay within the restrictions of the scale, we create **diatonic** seventh chords. The following example shows the diatonic seventh chords found within the C major scale:

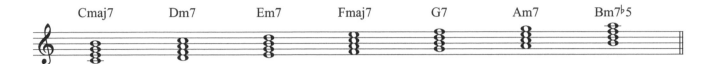

The **dominant seventh** chord—built on the 5th degree of the major scale—is perhaps the most commonly used seventh chord type in basic country and country blues. (The minor 7♭5 chord—built on the 7th degree—is rarely used in country music.)

Chapter 3

KEYBOARD HARMONY and VOICINGS

I n this chapter, we're going to work on getting some important keyboard "tools" under our fingers in all keys. This will help us to tackle the country comping patterns and techniques in the next chapter.

A **voicing** is a specific allocation of notes between the hands, chosen to interpret a particular chord. We'll start with basic right-hand voicings here, and then add the left hand a bit later.

Major triad inversions

We've seen how the major triad is constructed. Now let's look at inversions of the major triad, which are the basis for a lot of country comping styles. An inversion of a chord occurs when the sequence of notes from bottom to top is modified by moving one or more notes up or down by an octave. We start with the **inversions** of a C major triad:

TRACK 1

Note that in the above example, the triad appears first in **root position** (with the root on the bottom), then in **first inversion** (with the third on the bottom), then in **second inversion** (with the fifth on the bottom), and then again in root position, an octave higher. You should make it a goal to learn these inversions for *all* major triads, as follows:

TRACK 2

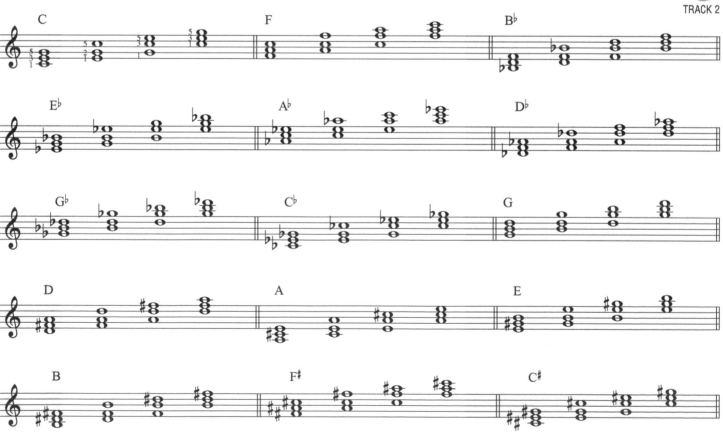

"Alternating eighth" and arpeggio patterns

We will now look at the "alternating eighth" pattern, based on major triad inversions. This is a right-hand device created by playing the upper notes in a chord on beats 2 and 4 of the measure (the "backbeats"), and playing the lowest note with the thumb on all of the upbeats (i.e., the "and" of 1, 2, 3, and 4), as follows:

It is valuable to have the inverted patterns under your fingers, as when we apply them to country progressions and songs, we will need to **voice lead** (i.e., connect smoothly between chords, without unnecessary interval skips). Here is the same pattern on all the remaining major triads moving around a **circle of 5ths** (a series of V–I relationships, e.g., C is the V of F, F is the V of B♭, and so on):

Now we will look at right-hand patterns using an **arpeggio** (an arpeggio is the notes of a chord played one at a time) or broken-chord style, again beginning with the C major triad:

Note the anticipation of beat 3, commonly used in country styles including bluegrass. Here is the same pattern on the next few major triads moving around a circle of 5ths. Again, you should strive to learn this in as many keys as possible:

TRACK 6

etc.

Major triads with octave doubling

Now we will apply "octave doubling" to these major triad inversions. This is done by repeating the lowest note of the triad an octave higher, creating a four-note voicing (instead of just three notes). This adds significant weight and power, and is a vital right-hand technique in rock, blues, and gospel, as well as in country music. First we will apply octave doubling to the inversions of a C major triad:

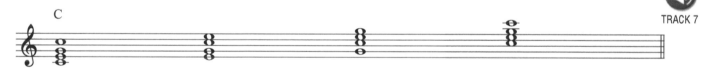

TRACK 7

Note that the root of the triad (C) is on the top and bottom in root position (the first and last voicings above), the 3rd of the triad (E) is on the top and bottom in first inversion, and the 5th of the triad (G) is on the top and bottom in second inversion. Fingering-wise for the right hand, I would suggest 1-2-3-5 for root position voicings, 1-2-4-5 for first inversion (I avoid using the 3rd finger here, as the middle interval is the largest), and 1-2-3-5 or 1-2-4-5 for second inversion. Again you should apply these inversions with octave doubling in all keys, as follows:

TRACK 8

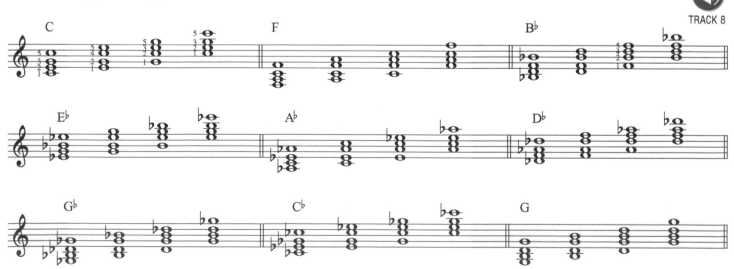

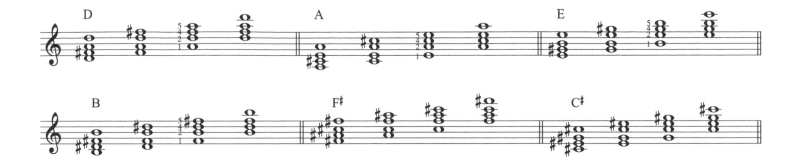

"Alternating eighths" and arpeggios with octave doubling

Now we will apply this octave doubling technique to the right-hand triad patterns developed earlier in this chapter, beginning with the "alternating eighth" pattern on the C major chord:

TRACK 9

Again, you should master this pattern in all keys. Here is the same pattern on all the remaining major triads moving around a circle of 4ths (a series of IV-I relationships, i.e., C is the IV of G, G is the IV of D, and so on):

TRACK 10

We can also make use of triads with octave doubling within the arpeggio patterns previously shown. Here is an example of this type of pattern, on a C major chord:

TRACK 11

Again note the anticipation of beat 3 in each measure, which is typical of this style. Here is the same pattern on the next few triads moving around the circle of 4ths (this is a great warmup and preparation for the bluegrass patterns we'll be exploring in the next chapter):

TRACK 12

NOTE: Inversions and patterns for **minor triads** can be easily practiced simply by flatting the 3rd of any previous major triad inversion or pattern (e.g., C = C–E–G, Cm = C–E♭–G).

Moving from chord to chord

You'll notice that some of the previous exercises were presented in a circle-of-5ths or circle-of-4ths sequence. Here is a diagram of the complete circle of 5ths or 4ths:

CIRCLE OF 5TH/4THS

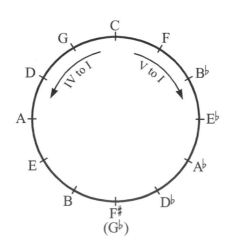

Note that we define clockwise motion to be a circle of 5ths, as it represents a series of V-I relationships (e.g., C is the V of F, F is the V of B♭, etc.), and we define counterclockwise motion to be a circle of 4ths, as it represents a series of IV-I relationships (e.g., C is the IV of G, G is the IV of D, etc). Many contemporary styles (including country) use chord progressions that move between adjacent stages on the circle of 5ths/4ths, making it a good tool with which to practice our inversions and patterns.

Let's try moving clockwise around the circle, a V-to-I movement (C–F–B♭–E♭, etc.). Here we are simply playing inversions of the chord tones (root, 3rd, 5th) in the right hand, together with the root of the chord in the left hand. This is a common voicing technique.

TRACK 13

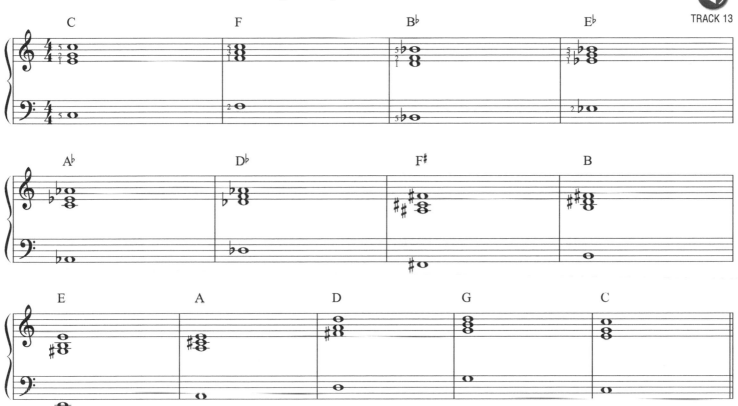

Note that in the first two measures, the right hand is playing a first inversion C major triad leading smoothly into the root position F major triad. This two-measure progression is a good example of voice leading, i.e., moving between chords using inversions, to avoid unnecessary interval leaps.

Next, try applying an "alternating eighth" comping style to these chord inversions:

TRACK 14

Also try an arpeggiated comping style:

TRACK 15

Now let's move the opposite way around the circle, a IV-to-I movement (C-G-D-A, etc.). Here we'll start at root position and alternate with first inversion. This two-measure pattern is repeated throughout the circle.

TRACK 16

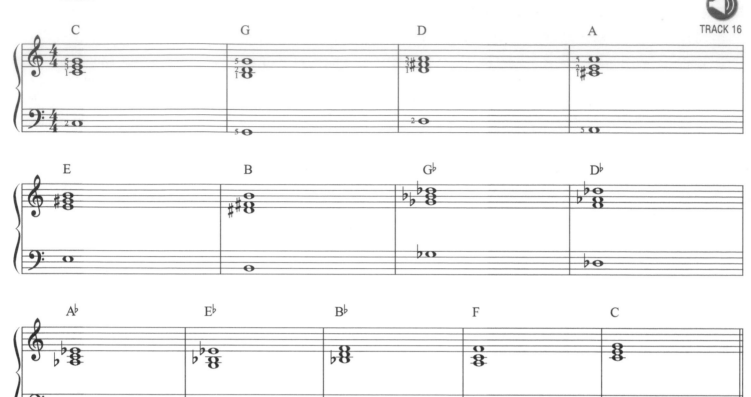

Again, we can apply an "alternating eighth" comping style to these chord inversions:

TRACK 17

We can also practice the arpeggiated comping style:

TRACK 18

Walkups and walkdowns

Next we will look at the "walkup" and "walkdown," which are staple elements in country styles. This is a great way to connect between chords moving around the circle of 5ths (V to I) or circle of 4ths (IV to I), particularly at the end of a phrase or song section.

NOTE: *We are using the terms "circle of 5ths" and "circle of 4ths" based on the assumption that the chord we are moving toward is always the "I" or tonic chord. However, the walkup and walkdown patterns will work the same, regardless of the function of each chord within the key.*

Walkups are used to connect between chords moving around the circle of 5ths, for example from C major to F major, a V-to-I progression in the key of F (which could also be a I-to-IV progression in the key of C).

The first stage in building a walkup pattern is to create a left-hand bass line. This will connect between the roots of the chords using scalewise movement, as follows:

Walkup stage #1

TRACK 19

The notes used to connect the C to the F are diatonic (i.e., belong) to both the C and F major scales. Next we will add a "moving tenth" line above this bass line. This is a right-hand line that is a tenth interval (octave plus a third) above the left-hand line, as follows:

Walkup stage #2

TRACK 20

Again all the notes in the above example are diatonic to both the C and F major scales. Next, we will add a "drone" note above these tenth intervals. "Drones" are repeated or held notes above moving lines or harmonies, and are widely used in rock and blues as well as country styles. When using a walkup, the drone will be the root of the first chord (C, in this case), which then becomes the 5th of the next chord, as follows:

Walkup stage #3

TRACK 21

At this stage, the pattern is sounding very "country"! Next we will add some eighth-note subdivision for the finishing touch. This is done by doubling the drone note (C) an octave lower, and playing it on the upbeats:

Walkup stage #4

TRACK 22

This is a very useful device to insert into a country comping pattern when this type of circle-of-5ths chord movement occurs (which is often). This is sufficiently important to practice in all keys, as follows:

Walkups around complete circle of 5ths, in all keys

TRACK 23

Next we will develop the various stages of the walkdown pattern. **Walkdowns** are used to connect between chords moving around the circle of 4ths, for example from F major to C major, a IV-to-I progression in the key of C (or I-to-V in the key of F).

The first stage in building a walkdown pattern is again to create a left-hand bass line. This will connect between the roots of the chords using scalewise movement, as follows:

Walkdown stage #1

TRACK 24

This is a mirror image of what we saw in stage #1 of the walkup pattern. Next we add a "moving tenth" line above the bass, as follows:

Walkdown stage #2

TRACK 25

Next, we again add a drone note above these tenth intervals. When using a walkdown, the drone will be the 5th of the first chord (C, in this case), which then becomes the root of the next chord, as follows:

Walkdown stage #3

TRACK 26

Finally we add some eighth-note subdivision by doubling the drone note (C) an octave lower, on the upbeats:

Walkdown stage #4

TRACK 27

Again, this is a very useful device to insert into a country progression when moving in a circle-of-4ths (IV-to-I) manner. As with the walkups, I recommend you learn the walkdowns in all keys, as follows:

Walkdowns around complete circle of 4ths, in all keys

TRACK 28

21

"Hammer" or "slip-note" techniques

Next, we will look at "hammer" or "slip-note" techniques for the right hand. This style was pioneered by the country pianist Floyd Cramer, in Nashville recording sessions during the 1960s. It is also sometimes referred to as a "fretted piano" style, as the piano is imitating the guitar technique of hammering on (i.e., playing a note and then altering the pitch by "hammering" onto a higher fret position with a left-hand finger). When combined with a "drone" or repeated note within a pentatonic scale, the results sound very authentically country. Here is a reminder of the C pentatonic scale:

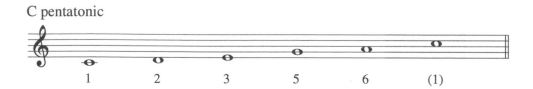

Next we isolate what I refer to as the "hammer-and-drone" points within this scale. The first drone note is the G, below which we can move between the notes D and E. If we "hammer" or move more quickly between these lower notes (while the upper drone note is still sounding), the desired stylistic effect is produced. Then the second drone note is the C, below which we can move between the notes G and A, as follows:

Note that the movement between the notes D and E below the drone of G, and the movement between the notes G and A below the drone of C, create alternating perfect 4th and minor 3rd intervals. These intervals create a very identifiably country sound. Note also that the drone notes are the tonic and 5th of the pentatonic scale. The drone notes are usually played with the pinky of the right hand, with the "hammer" notes underneath being played by the 2nd and 3rd fingers.

The hammer (or quick movement) below the drone is normally notated with grace notes, as in the following exercise using a C pentatonic scale:

In the first measure above, the drone note G (5th of the scale) is on top during beats 1 and 2. On beat 1, we "hammer" between D (the grace note) and E. Although it is common practice to notate the phrase in this way, in fact we normally want to strike the grace note (D) and the drone (G) *at the same time,* with the remaining hammer-on note (E) following shortly afterwards. On beat 2, we restrike the drone (G), this time above the pentatonic scale tones D and C. The drone note C (tonic of the scale) is then on top during beats 3 and 4. On beat 3, we "hammer" between G (the grace note) and A. On beat 4, we restrike the drone (C), this time above the pentatonic scale tones G and E. The second measure then repeats the same phrase, one octave higher.

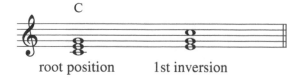

root position   1st inversion

Again, make sure that your right-hand pinky is always on the drones (notes with upward stems), with the 2nd and 3rd fingers playing the "hammers" below. Incidentally, you may notice with this fingering that your hand is actually in the same position used to play root position and first inversion triads, respectively. This is another way of seeing the above phrasing—as triad inversions ornamented by notes from the corresponding pentatonic scale.

As this phrasing is so widely used in country styles, I recommend that you learn it in all keys:

This "hammer-and-drone" pentatonic concept can also be applied within a sixteenth-note subdivision. This can be very useful in more modern country-ballad and country-rock applications, as follows:

TRACK 32

In comparing this example to Track 30, note that the movement below the drones is now using an even sixteenth-note rhythm (instead of the quicker "hammer" implied by the grace notes). This rhythmic variation should also be played in all keys, as in the preceding twelve-key pentatonic exercise.

In Chapters 4 and 5, we will see how pentatonic scales (incuding these "hammer-and-drone" phrases) can be used over different chords, for accompaniment and soloing purposes—stay tuned!

Dominant seventh chord inversions and patterns

While major triad inversions and patterns are by far our most essential tools in country music, it will also be useful for us to have the dominant seventh chord under our fingers in all keys and inversions. Note that each dominant seventh chord below is shown first in root position (with the root on the bottom), then **first inversion** (with the 3rd on bottom), then **second inversion** (with the 5th on bottom), and finally in **third inversion** (with the 7th on bottom).

TRACK 33

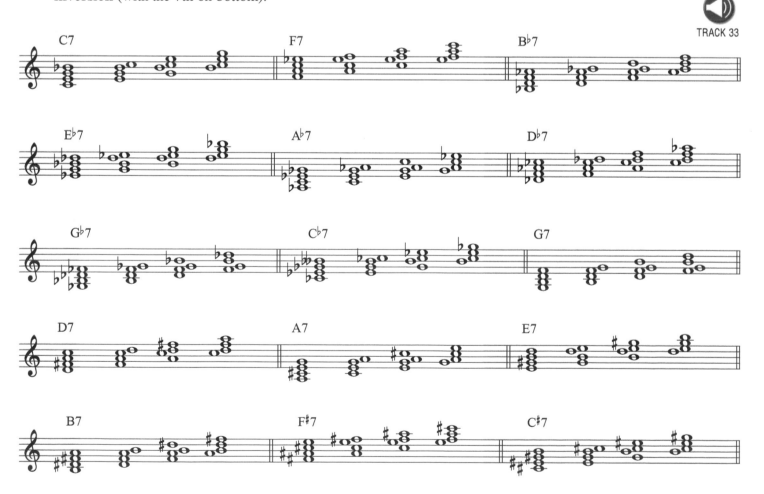

An "alternating eighth" right-hand pattern can be applied through all the inversions of a C7 chord. You should practice this pattern throughout the remaining keys:

TRACK 34

Next we will apply an arpeggiated right-hand pattern through all the inversions of a C7 chord. Again you should practice this pattern throughout the remaining keys:

TRACK 35

> NOTE: Inversions and patterns for **minor seventh chords** can be easily practiced by flatting the 3rd of the dominant seventh chord inversions and patterns (e.g., C7 = C–E–G–B♭, Cm7 = C–E♭–G–B♭).

Mixolydian patterns for country blues

Finally in this chapter, we will look at using Mixolydian modes to create country blues patterns. You'll recall that the Mixolydian mode is a major scale with a flatted 7th degree, and is a basic scale source for a dominant seventh chord. As blues music makes extensive use of dominant chords and Mixolydian modes, we would expect to find these devices used in hybrid styles such as country blues (as performed by Garth Brooks and many others). Here is a typical right-hand pattern using third intervals within a C Mixolydian mode, which could therefore be used over a C7 chord:

TRACK 36

The above pattern is useful to learn in all keys. Here is the same pattern on the next few dominant seventh chords, moving around the circle of 4ths (IV–I):

TRACK 37

In later chapters, we will see how to use these "Mixolydian thirds" to create two-handed country comping patterns, and also how to use other blues devices such as grace notes, half-step movements, etc., within a country blues framework.

Chapter 4

PROGRESSIONS and COMPING

Now we get to apply the keyboard harmony covered in Chapter 3 to create authentic comping patterns over chord progressions in a wide variety of country styles. We begin by reviewing the rhythmic subdivisions used in country music.

Rhythmic concepts

Most country comping uses patterns based around quarter notes or eighth notes. A simple quarter-note pattern would involve landing on beats 1, 2, 3, and 4 of a 4/4 measure, as in the following rhythmic example:

Quarter notes

TRACK 38

This basic rhythm is used in the older country styles such as cowboy music and Western swing, often at faster tempos. In later country styles such as bluegrass, honky-tonk, and Nashville (among others), eighth-note patterns were more common. It is important to understand that eighth notes can either be straight or swung. In **straight eighths**, each eighth note is of equal length and divides the beat exactly in half, as follows:

Straight eighth notes

TRACK 39

In a **swing eighths** rhythm, the second eighth note in each pair lands two-thirds of the way through the beat (equivalent to playing on the first and third parts of an eighth-note triplet), as in the following example:

Swing eighth notes

TRACK 40

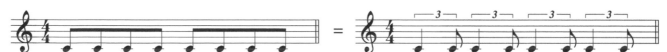

Note that the first measure above looks the same as the previous straight eighths example, but when a swing eighths interpretation (♫ = ♩ ♪) is applied to it, it sounds equivalent to the second measure above (the quarter-eighth triplets). However, as the second measure above is more cumbersome to write and to read, it is common practice to still notate as in the first measure above, but to rhythmically interpret in a swing eighths style as needed.

There will also be times when we need to land on all three parts of an eighth-note triplet. In this case, the swing eighths rhythmic interpretation will not work, as this only allows us to access the first and third parts of the triplet. Instead, we need to use either eighth-note triplet signs in 4/4 time or **12/8** time, which "exposes" all of the eighth notes without the need for triplet signs. The following example shows these two different notation styles:

Eighth-note triplets vs. 12/8 time

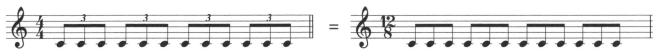

In the first measure above, each beat is divided into three equal parts. In the second measure, the time signature allows for twelve eighth notes into the measure, but we still subjectively hear four "big beats" at the start of each beamed group of eighth notes. The two measures are therefore functionally equivalent to one another. As a general rule, I would suggest notating in 4/4 time unless there are a lot of eight-note triplet signs needed (as in some Nashville styles, for instance), in which case, 12/8 time is less cumbersome.

Traditional country waltz

Our first country style is the traditional waltz, which was very popular in the cowboy period. Here is a typical chord progression used in this style:

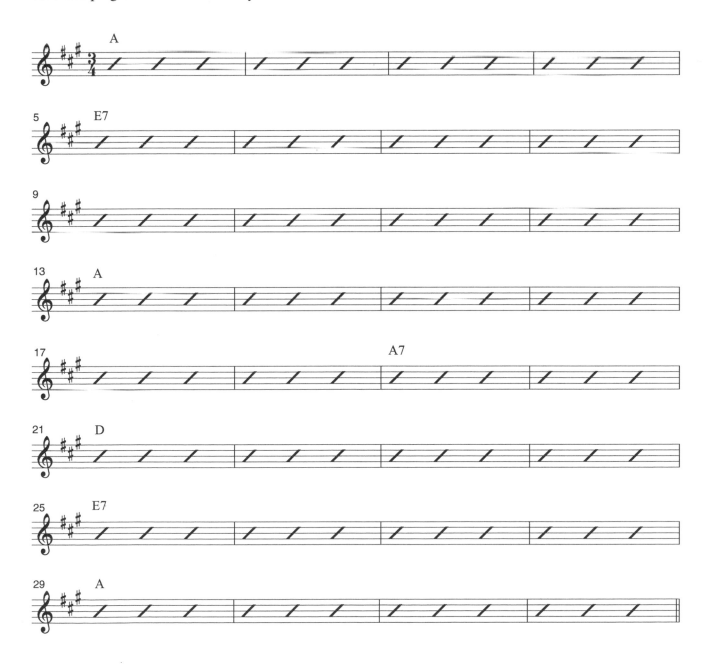

Now we will create a simple comping pattern using quarter-note rhythms and a mixture of triad and four-part voicings for each chord in the right hand. This pattern is in the style of "At Mail Call Today" by Gene Autry (an icon of the cowboy period). Note that even in this basic pattern, the right-hand chord inversions still need to voice lead (i.e., connect to each other without unnecessary interval skips):

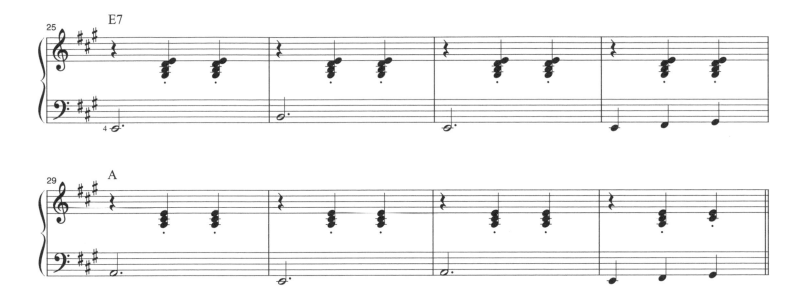

Note the alternating root-5th pattern used in the left hand, as well as the simple walkups in the last measure of each line, which add variation and movement. All the right-hand voicings are inversions of triads or four-part chords, except in measures 4, 16, and 32 where the note A is omitted from the A major triad to avoid a conflict with the G♯ in the left hand, and in measures 19 and 20 where the right hand is playing just the ♭7th, 3rd, and 5th of the A7 chord (this upper shape can also be thought of as a C♯ diminished triad, built from the 3rd of the A7 chord).

The "two-beat" feel

Next we will look at the traditional "two-beat," a 4/4 style also commonly used on songs from the cowboy period, as well as on Western swing tunes at faster tempos. The term "two-beat" here refers to the two main rhythmic pulses occurring on beats 1 and 3 in each measure, typically played by the bass in traditional country. Our pattern is based on the following chord progression:

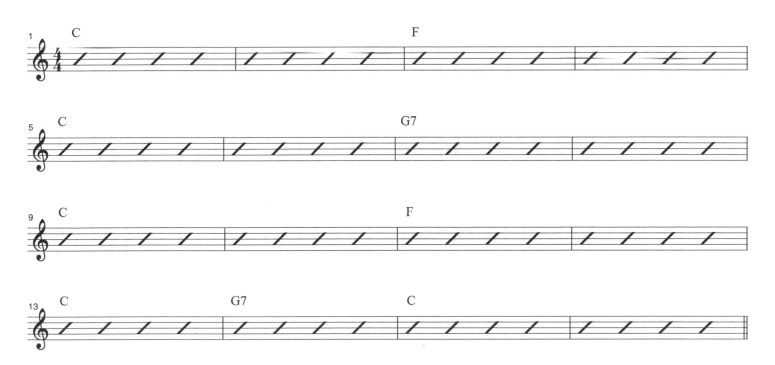

This comping pattern can be used for the traditional cowboy song "You Two-Timed Me Once Too Often" by Tex Ritter, as well as many other tunes from this period. The right hand is playing a triad or four-part chord on beats 2 and 4 of each measure. The left hand normally plays the root of the chord on beat 1 and the 5th of the chord on beat 3, except when a walkup pattern is being used to connect into the root of the following chord:

TRACK 43

The walkup and walkdown patterns in the even-numbered measures are similar to those in Chapter 3, except that they are in the left hand only. The right hand continues to play the chords on beats 2 and 4, rather than play a complementary walkup/walkdown part. This type of "left hand only" walkup/walkdown is common in the simpler country styles. Again we use voice leading in the right hand for a smooth and musical result.

Western swing

The piano feel for a lot of Western swing tunes is similar to the preceding "two-beat" feel, often with the addition of a top-note line in the right hand that acts as an instrumental countermelody. We will apply a Western swing comping pattern to the following chord progression:

This pattern is in the style of the tune "Yes Sir" by Milton Brown and his Musical Brownies. Note that all of the right-hand notes in each measure collectively create a triad or four-part chord as used in the previous comping patterns. However, there are now two parts being played by the right hand. The top note of the chord is played on beat 1 of the measure (or tied from the previous measure). The remaining (lower) notes are played on beats 2 and 4. Note that the top line often moves by half step (measures 10 -13). This adds some motion and melodic interest to the pattern.

TRACK 44

Bluegrass

Bluegrass tunes are normally played at medium-to-fast tempos and often feature intricate and melodic accompaniment patterns played by the banjo and/or mandolin. Although the piano is not commonly used in this style, we can adapt these patterns to the piano for comping purposes. We begin with the following chord progression:

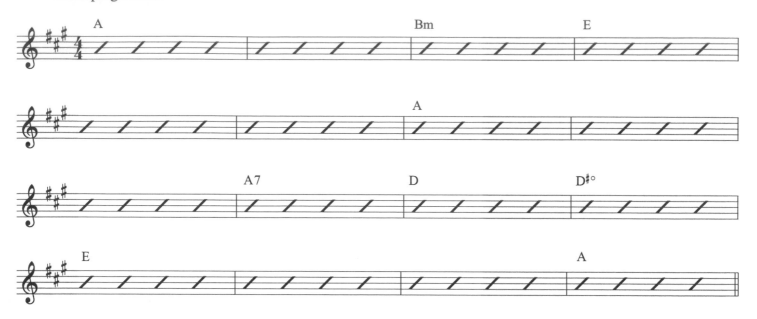

This progression is typically used for "Ballad of Jed Clampett" by Earl Scruggs and Lester Flatt, two of the most important pioneering figures of bluegrass. We will develop the piano comping pattern for this progression in three stages, and there are both slow and full speed versions of each stage to help you practice.

The first and most basic pattern uses triad voicings in the right hand; however, instead of just landing on beats 2 and 4 as in previous examples, the triad is "**split**" so that the lowest note lands on beats 2 and 4 and the remaining higher notes land half a beat later, on the "and" of 2 and 4 (a variation on the "alternating eighths" style learned previously). Meanwhile, the left hand is playing the root of the chord on beat 1, and another basic chord tone (3rd or 5th) on the "and" of 3, preceded by a connecting tone. This is a very good basic pattern for bluegrass, particularly at faster tempos:

Bluegrass stage #1

TRACK 45
slow

TRACK 46
full speed

For the next stage, we will develop an arpeggiated comping style. Those arpeggiated triad inversions you practiced back in Chapter 3 will now come in very useful! Note that the right hand is arpeggiating either a triad (with the top note "doubled") or a four-part chord, and is normally anticipating beat 3, which is a signature of this style. Meanwhile, the left hand has reverted back to a simple root-5th pattern on beats 1 and 3 of each measure:

Bluegrass stage #2

TRACK 47
slow

TRACK 48
full speed

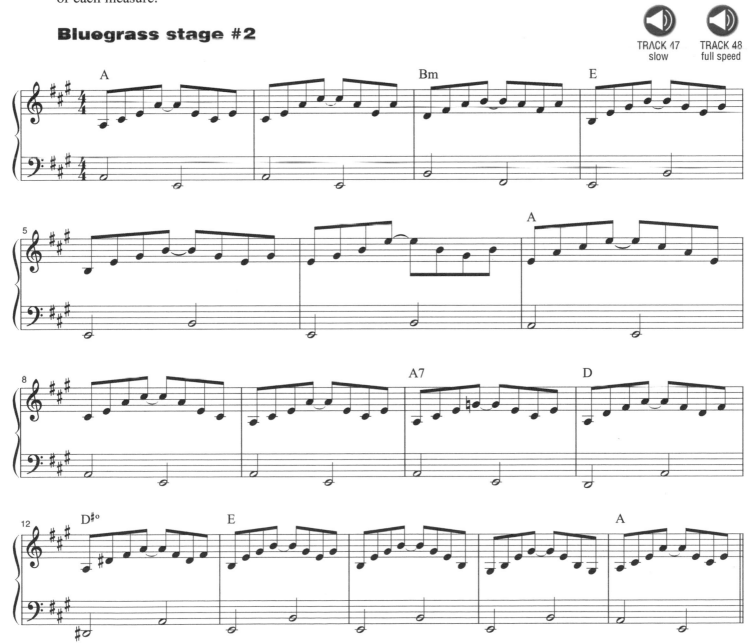

For the final stage, we will build a more intricate arpeggiated pattern reminiscent of the banjo picking style used in bluegrass. There are some technical challenges in adapting this type of pattern to the piano, particularly with the larger interval skips that require the right hand to rapidly change position, as follows:

Bluegrass stage #3

Note the following characteristics of the above pattern:

- In the first two measures (and the last), the right hand is playing the interval E-A (the 5th and root of the A chord) on beats 2 and 4. This strengthens the "backbeats" on the tonic chord.

- In comparison to the previous stage (#2), this pattern makes use of more chordal extensions (i.e., not just the root, 3rd, and 5th). On the A chord, we often add the 9th of the chord (B) between the root and the 3rd, and on the E chord, we add the 4th or 11th of the chord (A), often next to the 3rd (G♯). The E is a V chord in the key of A, and adding the tonic of the key (A) into the arpeggiated pattern on the V chord is a signature sound in bluegrass styles.

- Rhythmically, the right hand has more variation than in stage #2. Common rhythms include:
    - Six eighth notes followed by a quarter note (meas. 2, 3, 6, and 10)
    - Quarter note, followed by four eighth notes, followed by a quarter note (meas. 4, 5, 8, 12, and 13)
    - Anticipations of beat 3 (meas. 7, 9, and 11)

- There are some large interval skips in the right hand, often between beats 1 and 2 of the measure (this mimics the movement between strings on the banjo or guitar). You could actually play some of the low notes in the treble clef with the thumb of the left hand (for example, beat 1 in measures 4, 8, and 15) so that the right hand doesn't have to "jump around" so much.

- Otherwise, the left hand is playing a supportive pattern with the root of the chord on beat 1 and the 5th of the chord on beat 3. There are also some eighth-note "pickups," restating the root of the chord on the "and" of 2 or 4, and a walkup leading from the E chord in measure 15 back to the final A chord.

Honky-tonk/outlaw/country pop

We will now develop the "alternating eighth" comping style, which is suitable for many mainstream country songs, from honky-tonk and outlaw through to Nashville styles and beyond. We will start with the following chord progression, typically used for the Lefty Frizell tune "Long Black Veil":

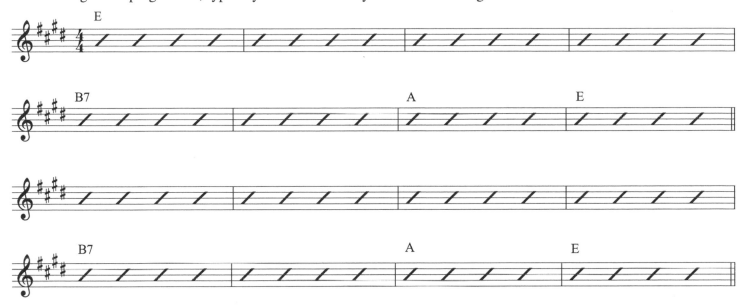

This is where your practice on "alternating eighth" patterns will really pay off! These patterns can be played with swing eighths or straight eighths. Many of the older or more classic country styles will use a swing eighths feel, as in the following example:

TRACK 51

Note the following characteristics of this comping pattern:

- The right-hand part is based on "alternating eighths" with octave doubling. Make sure that the right hand is in the correct position for each measure, with the thumb on the lowest note and the pinky an octave higher.

- Two-handed walkdowns are inserted into the comping pattern to connect between the A and E chords, in measures 7-8, and measures 15-16.

- Measures 9–16 introduce some different right-hand triad inversions. Again, we are voice leading between chord inversions to ensure smooth horizontal movement.

Nashville country waltz

Next we will develop a comping pattern for the Nashville country waltz, in the style of "He'll Have To Go" by Jim Reeves. The pattern for this smooth waltz style is similar to the preceding example but adapted for 3/4 time. Again the eighth notes are typically interpreted in a swing eighths manner in these older styles. Here is the chord progression typically used for this song:

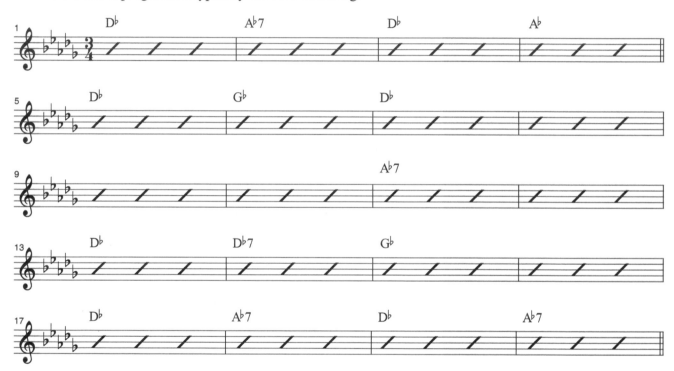

Note the double bar line used after the first four measures. This separates the intro (measures 1–4) from the rest of the song (beginning in measure 5). The "alternating eighth" waltz-style pattern is as follows:

TRACK 52

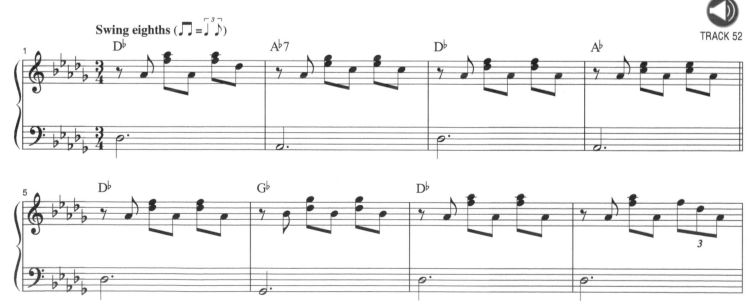

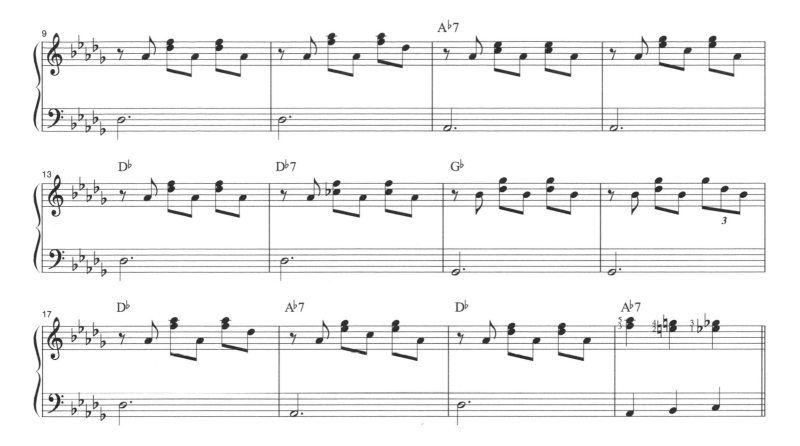

Note the following characteristics of this comping pattern:

- The right-hand part is again based on "alternating eighths" with some octave doubling. As before, you should keep the right-hand thumb on the lowest note in each measure (normally on the "and" of 1). Unlike the last pattern, however, this "thumb note" is not played on every upbeat; for example, in measure 1, the D♭ is played on the "and" of 3, in measure 2, the C is played on the "and" of 2 and 3, etc. The 2nd finger is normally the best choice for these notes.

- As a variation, the triad tones are arpeggiated (downwards) within an eighth-note triplet, during beat 3 of measures 8 and 16.

- A walkup variation is used in measure 20, with the right-hand part using third intervals and moving by chromatic half steps (i.e., a **chromatic third walkup**). This leads well into the tonic chord (D♭) if we are repeating back to the top.

Nashville arpeggiated 12/8 style

This is another very smooth, mid-tempo country style that emerged from the Nashville studios in the 1960s. We begin with the chord progression typically used for the Eddy Arnold classic "What's He Doin' In My World," as follows:

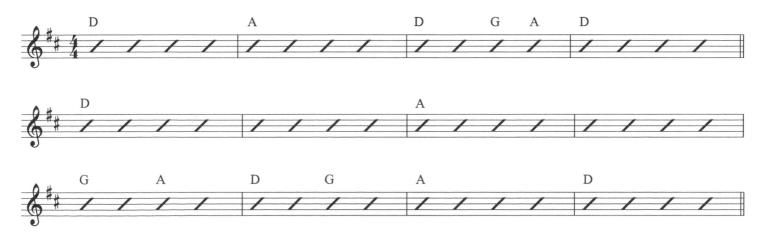

The intro (meas. 1–4) is again separated from the rest of the song with a double bar line. In the last measure of the intro, the pattern pauses on beat 1 and resumes on beat 4 with the eighth-note left-hand walkup. This is typical in intros from this period.

This comping style features a continuous arpeggio pattern in the right hand, which if notated in 4/4 would require eighth-note triplet signs throughout. So even though the preceding chord chart is shown in 4/4 time, we might choose to notate the actual comping pattern using 12/8 time to avoid having to write all the triplet signs (see discussion at the start of this chapter), as follows:

TRACK 53

Note the following characteristics of this comping pattern:

- The right-hand part is based on arpeggiated eighth-note triads with doubled octaves, adapted for 12/8 time. Different inversions are used within the same chord if it lasts for more than one measure, i.e., during measures 5–6 and 7–8.

- The left-hand part is mostly playing the root of each chord, with walkups and walkdowns between the I chord (D) and the V chord (A) during beat 4 of various measures.

Classic country rock

This style is associated with bands such as the Eagles, the Byrds, and Poco, who came to prominence in the 1970s. Musically, the patterns generally use a straight eighths rhythmic subdivision, at medium to fast tempos. This chord progression is typically used for the Eagles' tune "Lyin' Eyes":

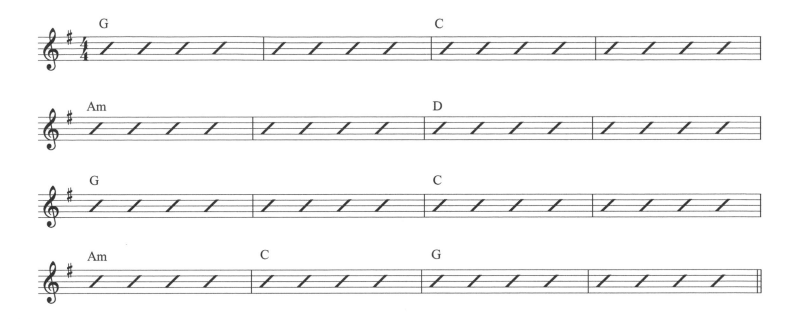

The first comping pattern we derive for this style is descended from the previous "alternating eighth" pattern we used for honky-tonk and outlaw, except we are now using a straight-eighths rhythm:

TRACK 54

Note that aside from a simple quarter-note walkup connecting the V chord (D) back to the I chord (G) in measure 8, we are using the "alternating eighth" right-hand triads over a root-5th pattern in the left hand. This is a very useful comping groove suitable for many country rock and country pop tunes from the 1970s onwards. Although we did not use octave doubling on the above triads, this could certainly be added to give some extra power and intensity to the feel.

The next pattern now uses pentatonic scale embellishments for a more up-to-date feel. This requires you to have the pentatonic "hammer-and-drone" exercises under your fingers (review Chapter 3 as needed):

TRACK 55

Note the following characteristics of this comping pattern:

- The beginning of the right-hand pattern for each chord resembles the previous "alternating eighth" style, with a rest on beat 1, the lower note played by the thumb on the "and" of 1, and then the remaining triad tones (this time with a "hammer" added) on beat 2. From that point in the measure onwards, drones are played by the pinky and generally land on the quarter notes, and the pentatonic movements underneath (with any "hammers") are played by the thumb and 2nd and 3rd fingers, using the eighth-note subdivisions. Within this general framework, there are many variations available.

- The top note in the right-hand part is normally one of the drones available within the pentatonic scale (tonic or 5th). For example, in measures 1 and 2, we're using the G pentatonic scale over the G chord, with the 5th (D) as the drone from measure 1 into measure 2, and the tonic (G) as the drone at the end of measure 2. Underneath these drones, we can then "hammer" or move between the lower notes of the pentatonic scale. We use the C pentatonic scale over the C chord in measures 3–4, and so on. (As explained in Chapter 3, you could also view these pentatonic ideas as ornamentations of the underlying chords. In measures 1 and 2, for example, we are playing within a G chord, in root position; then in 1st inversion. In measures 3–4, we are playing within a C chord in root position.)

- In measures 5–6, we are still using the C pentatonic scale in the right hand, this time "built from" the 3rd of the Am chord (more about "building" pentatonic scales from different parts of a chord, i.e., 3rd, 5th, 7th, in Chapter 5). As a variation, we're using the note A as a drone, which works well, as A is the root of the chord. The normal drone notes from the C pentatonic scale—the tonic (C) and the 5th (G)—would also work fine here.

- The left-hand part is a little busier compared to the previous pattern, with the root of the chord being repeated on the "and" of 2 as a pickup into beat 3, and additional connecting tone(s) being used in beat 4 of some measures.

In Chapter 5, we will take a further look at modifying country comping patterns by using pentatonic fills and embellishments—stay tuned!

Country rock ballad (eighth-note feel)

Country rock ballads can use either eighth- or sixteenth-note rhythmic feels. Here is the chord progression typically used for "Desperado," a country rock eighth-note ballad made famous by the Eagles:

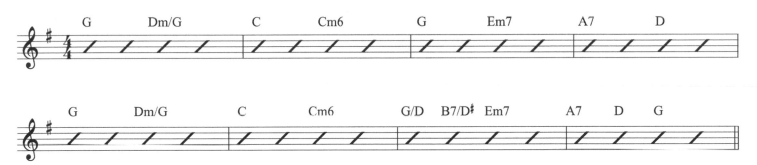

Note that the chords change more quickly than in some of the previous examples, i.e., we now have changes on beats 1 and 3 of each measure (with an additional chord change on beat 2 of measures 7 and 8). This busier "chord rhythm" is often found in ballad styles at slower tempos.

We can also use the sustain pedal on this comping pattern, as indicated. Ballad styles normally require the use of the sustain pedal during each chord—make sure you *release* the pedal at the point of chord change, and then depress the pedal during the next chord (before releasing any notes on the keyboard that you want to be "held"). A common mistake is to *depress* the pedal, rather than release it, on the point of chord change! Another way to put this is that you have an absolute point in time where you need to release the pedal, but a *time window* within which you then depress it.

TRACK 56

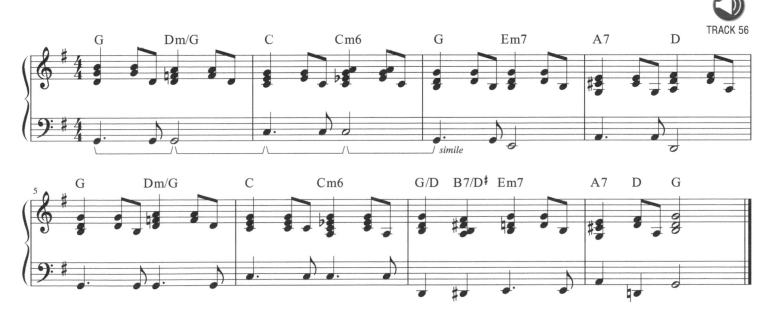

Note the following characteristics of this comping pattern:

- The right hand is playing a basic triad or four-part chord at the point of each chord change, inverted to voice lead smoothly from one chord to the next. Some "upper structure" triads are used, as follows:

    Dm/G: the D minor triad in the right hand is "built from" the 5th of G, creating an incomplete ninth chord that implies a suspended dominant quality.

    Em7: a G major triad in the right hand is "built from" the 3rd of E minor, creating an E minor seventh chord overall.

    A7: a C# diminished triad in the right hand is "built from" the 7th of the dominant A7 chord.

- During the first beat on each chord, the right hand is simply playing the quarter-note voicing. However, on the second beat, this voicing is "split," with upper notes being played on the downbeats (beats 2 or 4), and the bottom note being played by the thumb on the upbeats ("and" of 2 or 4).

- The left hand is mostly playing a basic "dotted quarter-eighth-half note" pattern common in eighth-note pop styles, except in measures 7 and 8 where the chords change more frequently.

Country rock ballad (sixteenth-note feel)

Next we will look at the country rock ballad using sixteenth-note rhythms. This more modern sound often borrows from R&B/pop stylings but with certain pentatonic devices that introduce the country element. Here is part of the chord progression typically used for "Victim of the Game" by Garth Brooks, a good example of this more contemporary country ballad style:

The comping pattern for this style now uses pentatonic fills within a sixteenth-note framework, as follows:

TRACK 57

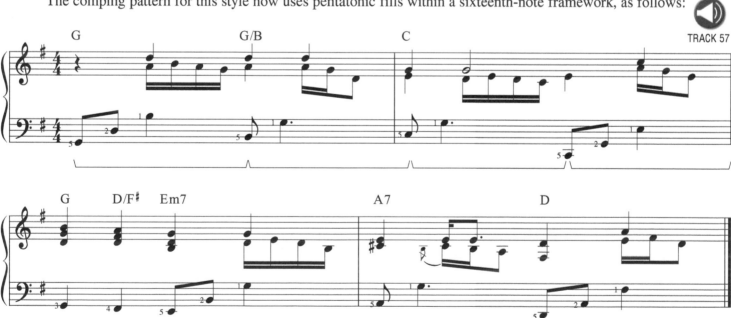

Note the following characteristics of this comping pattern:

- The left hand is normally playing either an "open triad" **root–5th–10th** arpeggio or an "incomplete" arpeggio (a good alternative when the hands are too close together to play the full open triad). All of these left-hand patterns are widely used in piano ballad styles.

- On beats 1 and 3 (normally the points of chord change), the right hand is usually playing a triad voicing or an "incomplete triad," i.e., just the 3rd and 5th of the chord on beat 1 of measures 2 and 4.

- During beats 2 and 4, the right hand is then playing sixteenth-note pentatonic fills below drone notes.

Measure 1: Over the G chord, the right hand is using a G pentatonic scale, and the drone or top note is the 5th (D).

Measure 2: Over the C chord, the right hand is using a C pentatonic scale and the drones are the 5th (G) and the tonic (C).

Measure 3: Over the Em7 chord, the right hand is "building" a G pentatonic scale from the 3rd of the chord, with G as the drone (more about "building" pentatonics from different chord tones in Chapter 5).

Measure 4: Over the A7 chord, the right hand is using an A pentatonic scale (with E as the drone), and over the D chord, a D pentatonic scale (with A as the drone).

Country pop "easy listening"

This style is very similar to "middle-of-the-road" pop music, and musically speaking it does not have many of the signature sounds we've so far developed for country styles. The comping patterns generally feature simple triads and eighth-note rhythms. Here is the chord progression typically used for "Feels So Right" by Alabama, a band identified with this urban cowboy or "easy listening" country style:

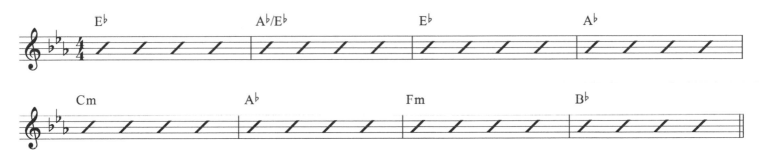

We can develop the comping pattern using right-hand triads and eighth-note arpeggios, as follows:

TRACK 58

Note the following characteristics of this comping pattern:

- The left hand is playing the root of each chord using a simple "dotted quarter-eighth" pattern, suitable for many pop and pop-rock styles.

- The right hand is playing a triad on the point of chord change (beat 1 of each measure), and different arpeggio rhythms towards the end of the measure.

- As indicated, the sustain pedal can be used towards the end of each measure to catch the arpeggio played in the right hand.

Country gospel

Many artists and bands have blended country and gospel styles together to great effect. A good example would be the Eagles' classic "Take It to the Limit," which uses the 3/4 time signature and eighth-note triplet rhythms commonly found in gospel music. Here is the chord progression typically used for the intro of this tune:

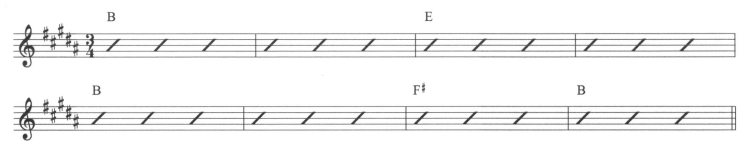

Our comping pattern for this style then blends country and gospel elements, as follows:

TRACK 59

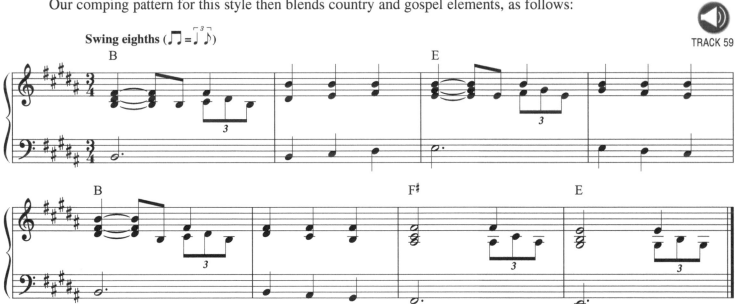

Note the following characteristics of this comping pattern:

- The right hand is playing a triad on the points of chord change (beat 1 of measures 1, 3, 5, 7, and 8).

- Both hands are playing a walkup pattern in measure 2, and walkdown patterns in measures 4 and 6. These are similar to the walkups and walkdowns introduced in Chapter 3 but adapted for 3/4 time. These patterns are prominently featured in gospel as well as country styles.

- Pentatonic fills are being used as follows:
  - Over the B chord (measures 1 and 5), the notes are from the B pentatonic scale, with an F♯ drone.
  - Over the E chord (measure 3), the notes are from the E pentatonic scale, with a B drone.

- The F♯ and E major triads are arpeggiated during beat 3 of measures 7 and 8, with the outer notes played on the downbeat followed by single notes during the eighth-note triplet.

Country blues

Finally in this chapter, we'll look at the blending of country and blues styles. Many contemporary country artists add a blues flavor to some of their tunes. This should not be surprising, as a lot of modern country music borrows from rock stylings, and the blues is an important ancestor of rock music. A good example of this type of artist is Garth Brooks, who successfully incorporates blues elements into some of his tunes. Here is a basic blues progression in the key of D, used for the Garth Books country blues tune "Two of a Kind, Workin' on a Full House," as well as many others:

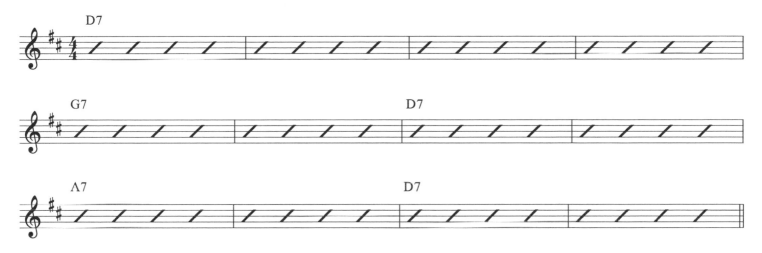

The first comping pattern will be based on the "Mixolydian third" patterns (using third intervals from Mixolydian modes). This is a good basic pattern for many blues styles including country blues:

TRACK 60

Note that the right hand in this pattern uses third intervals from the D Mixolydian mode over the D7 chord in measures 1–4, 7–8, and 11–12; thirds from the G Mixolydian mode over the G7 chord in measures 5–6; and thirds from the A Mixolydian mode over the A7 chord in measures 9–10.

Once you're comfortable with the basic Mixolydian patterns, you can start getting a little more creative with your country blues stylings. The next pattern still uses "Mixolydian thirds" but with added grace notes and "neighbor" tones moving into the 3rd or 5th of the chord by half step (i.e., ♭3–3 and ♭5–5), a signature sound in blues styles. The right hand is playing a full triad (instead of a two-note interval) at the start of each chord, and is using more rhythmic anticipations (landing ahead of the beat). The left hand is also busier with the use of eighth-note "pickups," i.e., playing on the "and" of 2 and 4, as follows:

Chapter 5
RIGHT-HAND TECHNIQUES for FILLS and SOLOS

In this chapter, we'll see how to add fills to country comping patterns and how to create improvised solos in country styles. The pentatonic scale is frequently used for country fills and solos, as are the major scales and Mixolydian modes.

Adding fills to comping patterns

We'll start out with a basic country I–IV–V chord progression as follows:

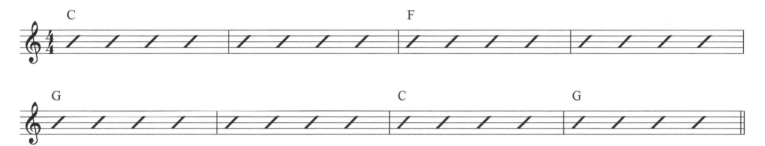

Next, we create a simple comping pattern using this progression, suitable for many honky-tonk, outlaw, and basic country pop tunes:

TRACK 62

Now we'll add fills to this comping pattern, using pentatonic scales and "hammer-and-drone" techniques first seen in Chapter 3. In this type of pattern, fills are often added just before a chord change. In the following example, we have added pentatonic fills in the right hand during beat 4 of measures 2, 4, 6, and 7, in each case leading into the following chord:

TRACK 63

We can further analyze the fills as follows:

- Over the C chord (meas. 2 and 7), the fill uses a C pentatonic scale, with G (the 5th) as the drone above the "hammer" notes D and E, played together with the note C as an eighth-note triplet.

- Over the F chord (meas. 4), the fill uses an F pentatonic scale, with C (the 5th) as the drone above G "hammering" into A, followed by G and F within the eighth-note triplet.

- Over the G chord (meas. 6), the fill uses a G pentatonic scale, with G (the root) as the drone above the "hammer" notes E and D, played together with the note B as an eighth-note triplet.

- A triplet subdivision has also been added to the right-hand walkup in measure 8.

Note that in each case the pentatonic scale chosen as the source of the fill has been "built from" the root of the chord, i.e., we used a C pentatonic scale over the C major chord, an F pentatonic scale over the F major chord, etc. Later we will see how to "build" pentatonics from different parts (i.e., 3rd, 5th, 7th) of the chord.

It's also important to apply these fills in the correct register, to ensure smooth voice leading—observing the surrounding chord voicings will help here. For example, the comping pattern in measure 2 had a root position C chord (with the note G on top), and so we chose G (the 5th) as the drone during the fill in beat 4. (Recall that each pentatonic scale has two drones, the root and 5th.) In measure 6, the comping pattern had a first inversion G chord (again with the note G on top), and so we again chose G as the drone during the fill in beat 4, this time as the root within a G pentatonic scale. It is vital to be able to insert fills below both of the drone notes—root and 5th—available within all pentatonic scales. Make sure you practice that twelve-key "hammer-and-drone" exercise back in Chapter 3!

Soloing with pentatonic scales

Next we will build some right-hand piano solos using pentatonic scales, over the same I-IV-V chord progression now transposed to the key of F:

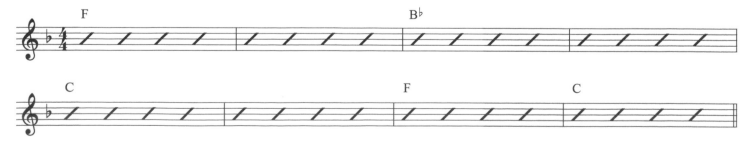

Our first solo (Track 65) uses triad voicings in the left hand, either as whole notes or landing on beat 1 and the "and" of 2. This works fine as a simple left-hand comp below the right hand. The right hand, meanwhile, uses pentatonic scales "built from" the root of each chord, i.e., the solo phrases in measures 1–2 are from the F pentatonic scale, the phrases in measures 3–4 are from the B♭ pentatonic scale, and so on. Notice the use of four-note (and three-note) pentatonic "subgroups," both ascending and descending, within the F, B♭, and C pentatonic scales. As an example, here are the four-note subgroups available within an F pentatonic scale (F-G-A-C-D), in ascending sequence:

TRACK 64

These groupings lay well under the right hand and can be applied in many ascending and descending patterns. Of course, there are a great many solo phrases that can be derived from the pentatonic scale, and the intervals in the scale lend themselves to the creation of melodic motifs. Although improvisation is always a creative process, keeping the following points in mind will help you create memorable solo phrases:

- Always think of solos as melodies in their own right (being spontaneously composed), rather than just "licks" or rote figures. Try to sing the solo as you play it. This increases the chances of creating something thematic, rather than just running up and down a scale.

- A great way to create melodies (and therefore solo phrases) is to start with a rhythmic phrase and then assign notes to each rhythmic event, from the scale being used. The following solo example mostly uses pairs of "swing eighth" notes, with some eighth-note triplets (i.e., during beat 3 of measures 1–4).

- Note that the rhythmic phrase in measures 3–4 is very similar to measures 1–2, but with different notes assigned to the rhythmic events. These musical sections (in this case, two-measure phrases) give essential "shape" to the solo, and again help it to sound more thematic. See what other combinations of notes you could assign to this rhythm, and then try it with rhythms of your own!

The track for this solo features a swing-eighths country pop rhythm section for you to play along with. You can practice the piano part along with the rhythm section (just turn down the right channel), and you can also improvise your own solo over the chord changes.

TRACK 65

Note that we also added a walkup within the solo in measure 8, leading back to the I chord (F major).

The preceding solo did not incorporate any drone notes or "hammer-and-drone" phrases within the pentatonic scales. These are now introduced in the next solo example, over the same chord changes:

This solo uses the same left-hand triad voicings and rhythms as the previous example. Again we are using the different drone possibilities (root or 5th) available within each of the pentatonic scales (with other scale tones being used below), as follows:

- Over the F chord (meas. 1 and 2): the drone is C (the 5th) within the F pentatonic scale.

- Over the F chord (meas. 2, beat 4): the drone is F (the root) within the F pentatonic scale, with B♭ used as a scalewise connecting tone between A and C, below the drone.

- Over the B♭ chord (meas. 3, beats 1-3, and meas. 4, beat 4: the drone is F (the 5th) within the B♭ pentatonic scale.

- Over the B♭ chord (meas. 3, beat 4, and meas. 4, beats 1-3): the drone is B♭ (the root) within the B♭ pentatonic scale.

- Over the C chord (meas. 5, beats 1-2, and meas. 6, beat 4): the drone is G (the 5th) within the C pentatonic scale.

- Over the C chord (meas. 5, beats 3–4, and meas. 6, beats 1-2): the drone is C (the root) within the C pentatonic scale.

- Over the F chord (meas. 7): the drone is F (the root) within the F pentatonic scale.

Note the rhythms in this example combine eighth-note triplets and rhythmic anticipations to good effect. Also, the half notes in measures 4 and 7 create space and "break up" the phrases for a more musical result.

Soloing with Mixolydian modes and grace notes

Next we will create a solo in a more country blues style using Mixolydian modes and grace notes, over the following progression containing dominant seventh chords:

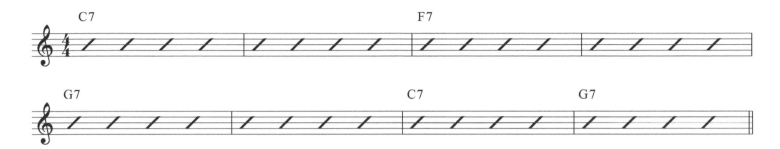

The following country blues solo based on this dominant chord progression has the "Mixolydian thirds" comping as a foundation, but with added grace notes and embellishments:

Note that the left hand is playing **root-7th** intervals on each chord. This is a common technique in blues as well as jazz styles. This interval is "range sensitive"—make sure you don't play it too low on the piano (it will sound too muddy) or too high (it will sound too thin). The range shown in the above example is good for this interval. The right-hand solo phrases can be analyzed as follows:

- Over C7 in measure 1, third intervals from C Mixolydian are used, with the added grace notes ♭3–3 (E♭ to E) and ♭5–5 (G♭ to G).

- Over C7 in measure 2, beat 2, A is moving to G below the drone C (all from C pentatonic), and the grace note A♭ is approaching the A by half step. During beat 4, the A (with double grace notes G and A♭) and C both "belong to" and are anticipating the next F7 chord.

- Over F7 in measures 3–4, third intervals from F Mixolydian are used, again with ♭3–3 (A♭ to A) and ♭5–5 (B to C) movements added. During beat 4 of measure 4, the B and D (preceded by the approach tones B♭ and D♭) "belong to" and are anticipating the next G7 chord.

- Over G7 in measure 5, the double grace notes A and B♭ lead into the 3rd of the chord (B), and the rest of the measure looks like a G pentatonic phrase using D as the drone, except the B has been replaced with B♭ for a "bluesier" sound.

- Over G7 in measure 6, beat 2, E is moving to D below the drone G (all from G pentatonic), and the double grace notes D and E♭ are approaching the E by half steps.

- Over C7 in measure 7, third intervals from C Mixolydian are again used, with the added ♭3–3 (E♭ to E) movement. The D and G on the "and" of 4 are anticipating the next G7 chord.

- Over G7 in measure 8, we are using a quarter-note right-hand walkup.

Using pentatonic scales over different chords

We will now explore how to build pentatonic scales from different parts of the chord (i.e., from the 3rd, 5th, or 7th). So far, we have simply built the pentatonic scale from the root of the chord (e.g., a C pentatonic scale over a C major chord) when creating fills and solos. Now we will explore some of these other options, as follows:

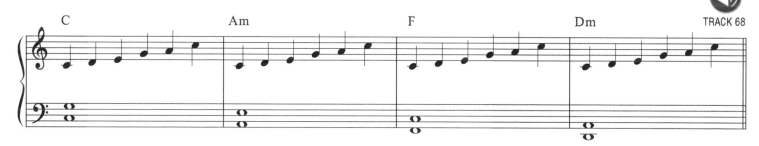

TRACK 68

In the above example, the left hand is playing simple root-5th voicings to define each chord. Each measure can be analyzed as follows:

Measure 1:   The C pentatonic scale is "built from" the root of a C chord. The scale degrees are the root, 9th (2nd), 3rd, 5th, and 6th (13th), with respect to the chord.

Measure 2:   The C pentatonic scale is "built from" the 3rd of an Am chord. The scale degrees are the 3rd, 11th (4th), 5th, 7th, and root, with respect to the chord.

Measure 3:   The C pentatonic scale is "built from" the 5th of an F chord. The scale degrees are the 5th, 6th (13th), 7th, 9th (2nd), and 3rd, with respect to the chord.

Measure 4:   The C pentatonic scale is "built from" the 7th of a Dm chord. The scale degrees are the 7th, root, 9th (2nd), 11th (4th), and 5th with respect to the chord. (Building a pentatonic scale from the 7th also works on a D9sus or D11 suspended dominant chord.)

Note that building the pentatonic scale from the higher chord tones (i.e., 5th and 7th) creates more upper extensions on the chord, and will therefore sound more sophisticated. We can summarize the above options as follows:

- On major chords, we can "build" a pentatonic scale from the root (basic sound as in first measure above), or from the 5th (more sophisticated sound as in third measure above.)

- On minor or minor seventh chords, we can "build" a pentatonic scale from the 3rd (basic sound as in second measure above), or from the 7th (more sophisticated sound as in fourth measure above.)

The influential rock and jazz pianist Bruce Hornsby (who started out with a country-based piano sound in the 1980s) uses this pentatonic "building" over different chords very effectively. We will now take the following diatonic triad progression in the key of C to use as a basis for this type of solo:

The following solo example repeats the same one-measure C pentatonic "hammer-and-drone" phrase throughout, superimposed over the different chord changes. Note the sixteenth-note rhythms and anticipations, giving a modern country/R&B ballad feel to the groove:

TRACK 69

In each measure above, the note G is the drone above the other notes from the C pentatonic scale (including the "hammer" notes D and E). This scale is used over the different chords as follows:

    Measure 1:   The C pentatonic scale is "built from" the 7th of the Dm chord.

    Measure 2:   The C pentatonic scale is "built from" the 5th of the F chord.

    Measure 3:   The C pentatonic scale is "built from" the root of the C chord.

    Measure 4:   The C pentatonic scale is "built from" the 3rd of the Am chord.

The left hand is playing basic root-5th (or root-5th-10th) whole-note shapes to define the chord. (Don't worry if you can't stretch the tenth interval in the left hand—just play the root and 5th of the chord.)

Now we will look at a chord progression in the key of F, which uses different pentatonic scales in the right-hand solo part. Again the same rules for "building" the pentatonic scales from different parts of the chord (i.e., root, 3rd, 5th, etc.) are being applied.

TRACK 70

Note that the right-hand phrasing is similar to Track 69, but this time different pentatonic scales are used, as follows:

> Measure 1: The C pentatonic scale is "built from" the 5th of the F chord.
>
> Measure 2: The B♭ pentatonic scale is "built from" the 3rd of the Gm chord.
>
> Measure 3: The C pentatonic scale is "built from" the 3rd of the Am chord.
>
> Measure 4: The F pentatonic scale is "built from" the 5th of the B♭ chord.

The tracks for these two examples have a rhythm section for you to play along with. After you've mastered these, go ahead and experiment with your own pentatonic ideas!

Using intervals within pentatonic scales

Now we will use intervals (two notes played together) within pentatonic scales as a source for fills and solos. Favorite intervals for this purpose are thirds and fourths. Using these intervals within pentatonic scales that are in turn used over different chords, gives some great-sounding results:

TRACK 71

Again we are "building" the C pentatonic scale from the root, 3rd, 5th, and 7th of the above chords respectively. Using these intervals within the scale (especially the fourth intervals) creates a modern and contemporary sound. We will now create another solo/fill passage over the earlier chord progression, using the above intervals within the C pentatonic scale:

TRACK 72

This creates a modern sound that would work in a more contemporary country/pop crossover context, as well in various R&B and funk styles. Again, you should experiment with your own pentatonic interval patterns when playing along to the rhythm section track provided.

Using "double fourths" within pentatonic scales

When we stack two perfect fourth intervals (one on top of another), we get a uniquely useful shape that I like to refer to as a "double fourth." A staple sound in jazz music, this is also used in some pop styles, including modern country rock. Again, Bruce Hornsby is noted for using this device as part of his signature sound. The pentatonic scale is a useful source of double fourths, as in the following example, which uses the double fourths found in the C pentatonic scale over different chords:

TRACK 73

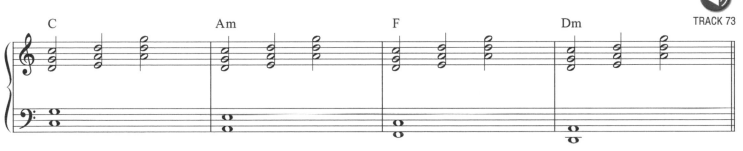

This is a great source of voicings when you want a different sound from the more conventional three- and four-part chords that we have been using in the right hand so far. When we then invert and arpeggiate these shapes, they work as a source for fills and solos. For example, the first double fourth shown above (the notes D, G, and C, from bottom to top) can be inverted and arpeggiated as follows:

TRACK 74

We will now invert and arpeggiate this double fourth shape (D, G, and C) and use it over the previous chord progression to create the following sixteenth-note solo example:

TRACK 75

This example uses just one double fourth shape; however, as we have seen, there are more double fourths available within the pentatonic scale. Have fun experimenting with these by playing along to the rhythm track!

Creating modern country rock solos

We will now use all of the preceding pentatonic techniques to create a modern country rock solo in the style of Bruce Hornsby. We begin with the following chord progression:

This is a simple progression that could be found in the keys of C or A minor. When playing a solo, it is common to repeat the chord progression a number of times (depending on how long the solo is overall). The following solo repeats the above sequence four times, creating sixteen measures in total. The rhythm section on the track has a bright, modern eighth-note country rock feel, and there are both slow and full speed versions:

TRACK 76
slow

TRACK 77
full speed

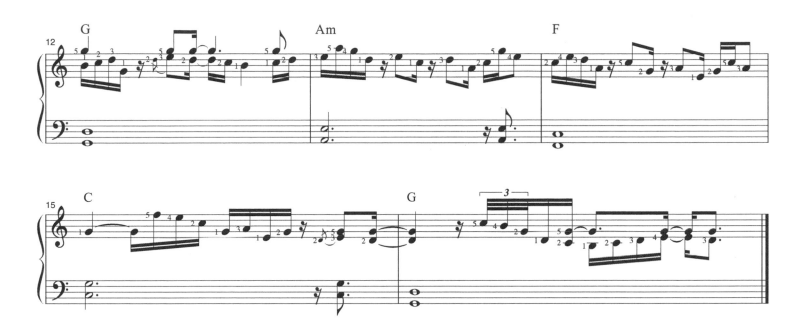

The left hand is playing simple root-5th voicings, outlining each chord. The right hand is using a mix of pentatonic scale runs, "hammer-and-drone" devices, third and fourth intervals, and arpeggiated double fourths and triads, as follows:

Measure 1:   Run using C pentatonic scale (built from the 3rd of the Am chord).

Measure 2:   Hammer-and-drone using C pentatonic scale (built from the 5th of the F chord).

Measure 3:   Run using C pentatonic scale (built from the root of the C chord).

Measure 4:   Hammer-and-drone using G pentatonic scale (built from the root of the G chord).

Measure 5:   Thirds and fourths within C pentatonic scale (built from the 3rd of the Am chord).

Measure 6:   Thirds and fourths within C pentatonic scale (built from the 5th of the F chord).

Measure 7:   Thirds and fourths within C pentatonic scale (built from the root of the C chord).

Measure 8:   Drone note of G, and run using G pentatonic, with the added note C (4th/11th of the G chord).

Measure 9:   Double fourth (E–A–D) arpeggiated, ending in run using G pentatonic (built from 7th of chord).

Measure 10: Hammer-and-drone using C pentatonic scale (built from the 5th of the F chord).

Measure 11: Hammer-and-drone using C pentatonic scale, then arpeggiated double fourth (D–G–C).

Measure 12: Hammer-and-drone using G pentatonic scale, with the added note C (4th/11th of the G chord).

Measure 13: Run using C pentatonic scale (built from the 3rd of the Am chord).

Measure 14: Run using C pentatonic scale (built from the 5th of the F chord).

Measure 15: Run using C pentatonic scale with the added note F, ending on hammer-and-drone phrase.

Measure 16: Run using G pentatonic scale with the added note C, ending on hammer-and-drone phrase.

Note that the pentatonic runs are sometimes supplemented with the 4th degree of the scale (e.g., adding the note F to the C pentatonic scale), often used to resolve to the 3rd.

Work on playing this solo with the rhythm section (starting with the slow tempo track if needed). Then try your own improvisations in the right hand over the root-5th voicings in the left hand, along with the track!

Chapter 6
STYLE FILE

In this chapter, we have seven tunes written in different country styles, and you'll get a chance to apply the piano techniques associated with each style. Most of the tunes have "comping" or chordal accompaniment sections using the patterns developed in earlier chapters, as well as sections containing more soloistic or ornamental right-hand passages. Note that in some country styles (e.g., bluegrass) the line between comping and soloing is often blurred: right-hand comping parts can still sometimes be busy and elaborate.

These tunes are all recorded with a rhythm section (bass and drums) as well as piano. On the audio tracks, the rhythm section is on the left channel and the piano is on the right channel. To play along with the band on these tunes, just turn down the right channel. Slow and full speed tracks are provided for each song.

1. Outlaw Country

The first tune is written in the style of "Long Black Veil" by the honky-tonk artist Lefty Frizell. The piece uses the "alternating eighths" comping style and a swing eighths rhythmic subdivision. This basic comping pattern works for a lot of honky-tonk, Nashville, outlaw, and country pop songs. The first chorus uses basic triads in the right hand and walkups in the left hand. The second chorus (starting in measure 17) adds octave doubling to the triads in the right hand, eighth-note "pickups" leading into beats 1 and 3 in the left hand, and both hands are now playing the walkups. This all helps to build momentum during the arrangement.

Make sure the right hand accurately swings the eighth notes as you alternate between the "thumb note" on the upbeats and the remaining chord tones on the downbeats. Also ensure that you observe the rests, as this is important to the style.

TRACK 78
slow

TRACK 79
full speed

2. The Foggy Mountain

The next tune is written in the style of the bluegrass tune "Flowers on the Wall" by the Statler Brothers. The straight-eighths rhythm and fast tempo are typical of bluegrass styles. The comping pattern in the first chorus uses "split" triad voicings in the right hand (the lowest note of the triad on beats 2 and 4, and the upper notes on the "and" of 2 and 4), while the left hand is playing the root of the chord on beat 1 and either the 3rd or 5th of the chord on the "and" of 3 (preceded by a connecting tone).

In the second chorus (starting in measure 17), the right hand is playing a bluegrass solo reminiscent of the arpeggiated picking style of the banjo. The arpeggios contain half-step movements such as $\flat$3–3 and $\flat$5–5 over the chords, and also require some abrupt register changes (at least for the pianist!). These techniques continue through into the ending section, starting in measure 33.

Imitating the banjo style here is technically challenging on the piano, particularly at faster tempos. Use the slower-tempo track as needed to get comfortable with the hand position changes before trying it at full speed!

TRACK 80
slow

TRACK 81
full speed

3. First Date

Next up, we have a tune written in the style of "Last Date" by the renowned Nashville pianist Floyd Cramer. This instrumental tune features the "slip-note" or "fretted piano" stylings that were his trademark. The piece has a mid-tempo, swing-eighths feel and is typical of the smooth pop-influenced country that came out of Nashville in the 1960s.

Note the use of "hammer-and-drone" figures in the right hand from the C, F, and G pentatonic scales (all built from the root of the respective chord). The left hand uses some root-5th patterns with eighth-note pick-ups, together with open and closed triad arpeggios. In the bridge section (measures 15–22), the right hand uses descending third intervals to support the melody.

Make sure the drone notes "sing out" in the right hand and are held for the correct duration. The hammers need to be articulated evenly below, and you can experiment with how quickly you play each grace note (shorter grace notes give a tighter sound; slightly longer grace notes give the hammer a "lazier" feel).

TRACK 82
slow

TRACK 83
full speed

4. Eagle Rock

The next tune is written in the style of "Lyin' Eyes" by the Eagles. This band were pioneers of the country rock sound that emerged in the 1970s and remains popular to this day. Straight eighths rhythms are predominant in this style, which combines the melodic flavor of country with the instrumentation and feel of rock music.

The piece starts out with a blend of "alternating eighths" comping, pentatonic "hammer-and-drone" devices, and arpeggiated or "split" triads in the right hand, together with some two-handed walkups. In the bridge section (starting in measure 17), the right hand melodically embellishes using descending sixth intervals and more arpeggios. In the end section (starting in measure 27), more fills are added, using pentatonic scale runs with sixteenth notes to increase the energy level.

The left hand is mostly playing the root and 5th of the chord on beats 1 and 3 of the measure, with an eighth note "pickup" into beat 3 (a very common pattern in this style). Again make sure that you bring out the drones on the top of the right-hand part, changing the hand position as needed to place the pinky on each drone note. Keep the eighth notes steady and even!

TRACK 84
slow

TRACK 85
full speed

5. Queen of Diamonds

Next we have a country ballad that has sections in both eighth-note and sixteenth-note rhythmic feels. The older country and country rock ballads (from the 1960s and '70s) tended to use more eighth-note subdivisions, whereas more recent country rock ballads (from the 1980s on) often use sixteenth notes.

The "eighth-note" section of this tune (measures 1–18) is written in the style of "Desperado" by the Eagles, one of their most famous and successful ballads. The right hand is playing a typical pop ballad pattern, which can be thought of as a variation on "alternating eighths" country comping—the right hand is still playing the upper chord tones on beats 2 and 4 and the lower tone with the thumb on the "and" of 2 and 4, but now a chord voicing is played on beats 1 and 3 (instead of a "thumb note" on the "and" of 1 and 3). The left hand is playing the root of the chord on beats 1 and 3, with some eighth-note pickups.

The "sixteenth-note" section of this tune (measure 19 onward) is written in the style of "Victim of the Game" by Garth Brooks. The right hand is again playing a chord voicing on beats 1 and 3, and a sixteenth-note figure during beats 2 and 4, often using "hammer-and-drone" phrases within pentatonic scales. Starting in measure 28, the right hand develops a soloistic character with more sixteenth-note arpeggios and pentatonic fills. The left hand is mostly playing open triad arpeggios (root–5th–10th) on each chord. Most of this is actually standard R&B/pop ballad piano, with the added pentatonic devices giving it a country twist.

Again, ballad styles normally require the used of the sustain pedal—release the pedal at the point of chord change, then depress it to hold the chord before you move on to the next harmony.

6. Playin' for Keeps

This is a country blues tune written in the style of "Two of a Kind, Workin' on a Full House" by Garth Brooks. As we saw in Chapters 4 and 5, there are some fun ways to incorporate blues piano stylings into your country comping and soloing. This tune has a swing eighths rhythmic feel and combines Mixolydian third patterns with two-handed walkups during the intro (measures 1–4). In the first chorus (starting in measure 5), the comping pattern continues with the Mixolydian thirds and grace notes, with a lot of ♭3–3 movement on the chords, which is a signature of blues styles. The left hand is underpinning all this with a typical country bass line, landing on beats 1 and 3 with some eighth-note pickups.

A country-blues solo is developed over the second chorus (starting in measure 17). This uses Mixolydian modes (triads, third intervals, and single lines), drone notes, and more rhythmic upbeats and eighth-note triplets. Have fun putting the blues into your country music!

TRACK 88
slow

TRACK 89
full speed

7. The Valley Trail

Our last tune is written in the modern country rock style of "The Valley Road" by Bruce Hornsby. The piece features a blend of country, rock, and jazz piano techniques for which Hornsby is particularly noted. The song form is ABAB, with a comping groove and fills over the first A and B sections, and a piano solo over the second A and B sections. The piano solo then continues over the end section of the tune.

In the first A section (starting in measure 1), the right hand is playing a mixture of double fourth shapes, triads and pentatonic "hammer-and-drone" phrases. The double fourths add a jazz color and have a transparent and modern sound. The left hand is playing a root-5th and root-6th pattern borrowed from blues and rock styles. Then in the first B section (starting in measure 17), the right hand is playing triads on each chord, with some top-note movement and pentatonic fills. The left hand is generally playing the chord roots on beats 1 and/or 3, with some pickups and anticipations.

In the second A section (starting in measure 25), we have a Hornsby-style piano solo, with arpeggiated double fourths and triads, pentatonic runs and "hammer-and-drone" phrases, descending sixth interval patterns, sixteenth-note upbeats and syncopation, and so on. The solo continues into the second B section (starting in measure 41) and into the end section (starting in measure 49), where fourth intervals from the A pentatonic scale are added into the mix.

As with most repetitive rock and blues-styled left-hand parts, you should practice this left hand (root-5th and root-6th) pattern until it becomes automatic. That way, you'll be better able to focus on all the cool stuff going on with the right hand. Enjoy!

*Chord symbols reflect basic harmony throughout.

KEYBOARD STYLE SERIES

THE COMPLETE GUIDE!

These book/audio packs provide focused lessons that contain valuable how-to insight, essential playing tips, and beneficial information for all players. From comping to soloing, comprehensive treatment is given to each subject. The companion audio features many of the examples in the book performed either solo or with a full band.

BEBOP JAZZ PIANO
by John Valerio

This book provides detailed information for bebop and jazz keyboardists on: chords and voicings, harmony and chord progressions, scales and tonality, common melodic figures and patterns, comping, characteristic tunes, the styles of Bud Powell and Thelonious Monk, and more.

00290535 Book/Online Audio $21.99

BEGINNING ROCK KEYBOARD
by Mark Harrison

This comprehensive book/audio package will teach you the basic skills needed to play beginning rock keyboard. From comping to soloing, you'll learn the theory, the tools, and the techniques used by the pros. The accompanying audio demonstrates most of the music examples in the book.

00311922 Book/Online Audio $16.99

BLUES PIANO
by Mark Harrison

With this book/audio pack, you'll learn the theory, the tools, and even the tricks that the pros use to play the blues. Covers: scales and chords; left-hand patterns; walking bass; endings and turnarounds; right-hand techniques; how to solo with blues scales; crossover licks; and more.

00311007 Book/Online Audio $22.99

BOOGIE-WOOGIE PIANO
by Todd Lowry

From learning the basic chord progressions to inventing your own melodic riffs, you'll learn the theory, tools and techniques used by the genre's best practicioners.

00117067 Book/Online Audio $17.99

BRAZILIAN PIANO
by Robert Willey and Alfredo Cardim

Brazilian Piano teaches elements of some of the most appealing Brazilian musical styles: choro, samba, and bossa nova. It starts with rhythmic training to develop the fundamental groove of Brazilian music.

00311469 Book/Online Audio $19.99

CONTEMPORARY JAZZ PIANO
by Mark Harrison

From comping to soloing, you'll learn the theory, the tools, and the techniques used by the pros. The full band tracks on the audio feature the rhythm section on the left channel and the piano on the right channel, so that you can play along with the band.

00311848 Book/Online Audio $19.99

COUNTRY PIANO
by Mark Harrison

Learn the theory, the tools, and the tricks used by the pros to get that authentic country sound. This book/audio pack covers: scales and chords, walkup and walkdown patterns, comping in traditional and modern country, Nashville "fretted piano" techniques and more.

00311052 Book/Online Audio $19.99

GOSPEL PIANO
by Kurt Cowling

Discover the tools you need to play in a variety of authentic gospel styles, through a study of rhythmic devices, grooves, melodic and harmonic techniques, and formal design. The accompanying audio features over 90 tracks, including piano examples as well as the full gospel band.

00311327 Book/Online Adio $19.99

INTRO TO JAZZ PIANO
by Mark Harrison

From comping to soloing, you'll learn the theory, the tools, and the techniques used by the pros. The accompanying audio demonstrates most of the music examples in the book. The full band tracks feature the rhythm section on the left channel and the piano on the right channel, so that you can play along with the band.

00312088 Book/Online Audio $19.99

JAZZ-BLUES PIANO
by Mark Harrison

This comprehensive book will teach you the basic skills needed to play jazz-blues piano. Topics covered include: scales and chords • harmony and voicings • progressions and comping • melodies and soloing • characteristic stylings.

00311243 Book/Online Audio $19.99

JAZZ-ROCK KEYBOARD
by T. Lavitz

Learn what goes into mixing the power and drive of rock music with the artistic elements of jazz improvisation in this comprehensive book and CD package. This instructional tool delves into scales and modes, and how they can be used with various chord progressions to develop the best in soloing chops.

00290536 Book/CD Pack..................................$17.95

LATIN JAZZ PIANO
by John Valerio

This book is divided into three sections. The first covers Afro-Cuban (Afro-Caribbean) jazz, the second section deals with Brazilian influenced jazz – Bossa Nova and Samba, and the third contains lead sheets of the tunes and instructions for the play-along audio.

00311345 Book/Online Audio $19.99

MODERN POP KEYBOARD
by Mark Harrison

From chordal comping to arpeggios and ostinatos, from grand piano to synth pads, you'll learn the theory, the tools, and the techniques used by the pros. The online audio demonstrates most of the music examples in the book.

00146596 Book/Online Audio $19.99

NEW AGE PIANO
by Todd Lowry

From melodic development to chord progressions to left-hand accompaniment patterns, you'll learn the theory, the tools and the techniques used by the pros. The accompanying 96-track CD demonstrates most of the music examples in the book.

00117322 Book/CD Pack..................................$16.99

POST-BOP JAZZ PIANO
by John Valerio

This book/audio pack will teach you the basic skills needed to play post-bop jazz piano. Learn the theory, the tools, and the tricks used by the pros to play in the style of Bill Evans, Thelonious Monk, Herbie Hancock, McCoy Tyner, Chick Corea and others. Topics covered include: chord voicings, scales and tonality, modality, and more.

00311005 Book/Online Audio $19.99

PROGRESSIVE ROCK KEYBOARD
by Dan Maske

You'll learn how soloing techniques, form, rhythmic and metrical devices, harmony, and counterpoint all come together to make this style of rock the unique and exciting genre it is.

00311307 Book/Online Audio $19.99

R&B KEYBOARD
by Mark Harrison

From soul to funk to disco to pop, you'll learn the theory, the tools, and the tricks used by the pros with this book/audio pack. Topics covered include: scales and chords, harmony and voicings, progressions and comping, rhythmic concepts, characteristic stylings, the development of R&B, and more! Includes seven songs.

00310881 Book/Online Audio $22.99

ROCK KEYBOARD
by Scott Miller

Learn to comp or solo in any of your favorite rock styles. Listen to the audio to hear your parts fit in with the total groove of the band. Includes 99 tracks! Covers: classic rock, pop/rock, blues rock, Southern rock, hard rock, progressive rock, alternative rock and heavy metal.

00310823 Book/Online Audio $17.99

ROCK 'N' ROLL PIANO
by Andy Vinter

Take your place alongside Fats Domino, Jerry Lee Lewis, Little Richard, and other legendary players of the '50s and '60s! This book/audio pack covers: left-hand patterns; basic rock 'n' roll progressions; right-hand techniques; straight eighths vs. swing eighths; glisses, crushed notes, rolls, note clusters and more. Includes six complete tunes.

00310912 Book/Online Audio $19.99

SALSA PIANO
by Hector Martignon

From traditional Cuban music to the more modern Puerto Rican and New York styles, you'll learn the all-important rhythmic patterns of salsa and how to apply them to the piano. The book provides historical, geographical and cultural background info, and the 50+-tracks includes piano examples and a full salsa band percussion section.

00311049 Book/Online Audio $19.99

SMOOTH JAZZ PIANO
by Mark Harrison

Learn the skills you need to play smooth jazz piano – the theory, the tools, and the tricks used by the pros. Topics covered include: scales and chords; harmony and voicings; progressions and comping; rhythmic concepts; melodies and soloing; characteristic stylings; discussions on jazz evolution.

00311095 Book/Online Audio $19.99

STRIDE & SWING PIANO
by John Valerio

Learn the styles of the stride and swing piano masters, such as Scott Joplin, Jimmy Yancey, Pete Johnson, Jelly Roll Morton, James P. Johnson, Fats Waller, Teddy Wilson, and Art Tatum. This book/audio pack covers classic ragtime, early blues and boogie woogie, New Orleans jazz and more. Includes 14 songs.

00310882 Book/Online Audio $22.99

WORSHIP PIANO
by Bob Kauflin

From chord inversions to color tones, from rhythmic patterns to the Nashville Numbering System, you'll learn the tools and techniques needed to play piano or keyboard in a modern worship setting.

00311425 Book/Online Audio $19.99

HAL•LEONARD®

Prices, contents, and availability
subject to change without notice.

www.halleonard.com

TOP COUNTRY HITS
Arranged for piano and voice with guitar chords.

Top Country Hits of 2019-2020
18 of the best country songs from 2019 to 2020: All to Myself • Beer Never Broke My Heart • The Bones • Even Though I'm Leaving • Girl • God's Country • I Don't Know About You • Look What God Gave Her • Miss Me More • Old Town Road (Remix) • One Man Band • One Thing Right • Prayed for You • Rainbow • Remember You Young • 10,000 Hours • What If I Never Get over You • Whiskey Glasses.
00334223...$17.99

Top Country Hits of 2018-2019
18 Hot Singles
18 of the year's hottest country hits arranged for piano, voice and guitar. Includes: Best Shot (Jimmie Allen) • Drowns the Whiskey (Jason Aldean) • Get Along (Kenny Chesney) • Hangin' On (Chris Young) • Heaven (Kane Brown) • Love Wins (Carrie Underwood) • Mercy (Brett Young) • Rich (Maren Morris) • She Got the Best of Me (Luke Combs) • Simple (Florida Georgia Line) • Up Down (Morgan Wallen feat. Florida Georgia Line) • and more.
00289814...$17.99

Top Country Hits of 2017-2018
18 of the year's top toe-tapping, twangy hits: Body like a Back Road • Broken Halos • Craving You • Dear Hate • Dirt on My Boots • Dirty Laundry • Drinkin' Problem • Fighter • Hurricane • Legends • Meant to Be • Millionaire • Yours • and more.
00267160...$17.99

Top Country Hits of 2015-2016
14 of the year's most popular country songs: Burning House (Cam) • Biscuits (Kacey Musgraves) • Girl Crush (Little Big Town) • I'm Comin' Over (Chris Young) • Let Me See You Girl (Cole Swindell) • Smoke Break (Carrie Underwood) • Strip It Down (Luke Bryan) • Take Your Time (Sam Hunt) • Traveller (Chris Stapleton) • and more.
00156297...$16.99

Top Country Hits of 2014-2015
14 of the year's most popular country songs. Includes: American Kids (Kenny Chesney) • Day Drinking (Little Big Town) • I See You (Luke Bryan) • Neon Light (Blake Shelton) • Payback (Rascal Flatts) • Shotgun Rider (Tim McGraw) • Something in the Water (Carrie Underwood) • Sunshine & Whiskey (Frankie Ballard) • Talladega (Eric Church) • and more.
00142574...$16.99

Top Country Hits of 2013-2014
15 of today's most recognizable hits from country's hottest stars, including: Carolina (Parmalee) • Cruise (Florida Georgia Line) • Drunk Last Night (Eli Young Band) • Mine Would Be You (Blake Shelton) • Southern Girl (Tim McGraw) • That's My Kind of Night (Luke Bryan) • We Were Us (Keith Urban and Miranda Lambert) • and more.
00125359...$16.99

Top Country Hits of 2012-2013
Features 15 fantastic country hits: Beer Money • Begin Again • Better Dig Two • Come Wake Me Up • Every Storm (Runs Out of Rain) • Fastest Girl in Town • Hard to Love • Kiss Tomorrow Goodbye • The One That Got Away • Over You • Red • Take a Little Ride • Til My Last Day • Wanted • We Are Never Ever Getting Back Together.
00118291...$14.99

HAL•LEONARD®

Prices, content and availability subject to change without notice.

BIG BOOKS of Music

Arrangements for piano, voice, and guitar in books with stay-open binding, so the books lie flat without breaking the spine.

     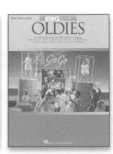 

BIG BOOK OF BALLADS

62 songs: Candle in the Wind • City of Stars • (Everything I Do) I Do It for You • I Write the Songs • Moon River • Tears in Heaven • A Thousand Years • What a Wonderful World • You've Got a Friend • and more!
00357998 ....$32.99

BIG BOOK OF BLUEGRASS SONGS

70 songs: Alabama Jubilee • Blue Moon of Kentucky • Dark Holler • I Am a Man of Constant Sorrow • Mule Skinner Blues • Orange Blossom Special • Rocky Top • Wildwood Flower • and more.
00311484 ....$22.99

BIG BOOK OF BLUES

80 songs: Baby Please Don't Go • Caldonia • I'm a Man • Kansas City • Milk Cow Blues • Reconsider Baby • Wang Dang Doodle • You Shook Me • and scores more.
00311843 ....$19.99

BIG BOOK OF BROADWAY

70 songs: All I Ask of You (from *The Phantom of the Opera*) • Bali Ha'i (from *South Pacific*) • Bring Him Home (from *Les Misérables*) • Burn (from *Hamilton*) • Luck Be a Lady (from *Guys and Dolls*) • One (from *A Chorus Line*) • Seasons of Love (from *Rent*) • and more!
00299346 ....$32.99

BIG BOOK OF CHILDREN'S SONGS

55 songs: Camptown Races • (Oh, My Darling) Clementine • Do-Re-Mi • Eensy Weensy Spider • Hickory Dickory Dock • Humpty Dumpty • John Jacob Jingleheimer Schmidt • Mickey Mouse March • Pop Goes the Weasel • This Land Is Your Land • Yellow Submarine • more!
00359261 ....$17.99

BIG BOOK OF CHRISTMAS SONGS

126 songs: Away in a Manger • Carol of the Bells • Good King Wenceslas • It Came upon the Midnight Clear • Joy to the World • O Holy Night • The Twelve Days of Christmas • We Wish You a Merry Christmas • and more.
00311520 ....$22.99

BIG BOOK OF CONTEMPORARY CHRISTIAN FAVORITES

50 songs: Big House • Follow You • I Still Believe • Let Us Pray • More Beautiful You • People Need the Lord • Sing, Sing, Sing • Thy Word • What Are You Waiting For • You Reign • and many more.
00312067 ....$21.99

BIG BOOK OF FOLKSONGS

125 songs: Cotton Eyed Joe • Down by the Salley Gardens • Frere Jacques (Are You Sleeping?) • Hatikvah • Mexican Hat Dance • Sakura • Simple Gifts • Song of the Volga Boatman • The Water Is Wide • and many more.
00312549 ....$24.99

BIG BOOK OF FRENCH SONGS

70 songs: April in Paris • Autumn Leaves • Beyond the Sea • Can Can • I Dreamed a Dream • La Marseillaise • My Man (Mon Homme) • Sand and Sea • Un Grand Amour (More, More & More) • Where Is Your Heart • and more.
00311154 ....$27.99

BIG BOOK OF GERMAN SONGS

78 songs: Ach, Du Lieber Augustin • Ave Maria • Bist Du Bei Mir • O Tannenbaum • Pizzicato Polka • Ständchen • Vilja Lied • and dozens more!
00311816 ....$24.99

BIG BOOK OF GOSPEL SONGS

100 songs: Amazing Grace • Because He Lives • Give Me That Old Time Religion • His Eye Is on the Sparrow • I Saw the Light • My Tribute • The Old Rugged Cross • Precious Lord, Take My Hand • There Is Power in the Blood • Will the Circle Be Unbroken • and more!
00310604 ....$22.99

BIG BOOK OF HYMNS

125 songs: Blessed Assurance • For the Beauty of the Earth • Holy, Holy, Holy • It Is Well with My Soul • Just As I Am • A Mighty Fortress Is Our God • The Old Rugged Cross • What a Friend We Have in Jesus • and more.
00310510 ....$22.99

BIG BOOK OF IRISH SONGS

75 songs: Danny Boy • The Irish Washerwoman • Jug of Punch • Molly Malone • My Wild Irish Rose • Peg O' My Heart • 'Tis the Last Rose of Summer • Too-Ra-Loo-Ra-Loo-Ra (That's an Irish Lullaby) • When Irish Eyes Are Smiling • and more.
00310981 ....$19.99

BIG BOOK OF ITALIAN FAVORITES

80 songs: Carnival of Venice • Funiculi Funicula • Italian National Anthem • La Donna É Mobile • Mambo Italiano • Mona Lisa • O Mio Babbino Caro • Speak Softly, Love • Tarantella • That's Amore • and more!
00311185 ....$24.99

BIG BOOK OF JAZZ

75 songs: Autumn Leaves • Days of Wine and Roses • Falling in Love with Love • Honeysuckle Rose • I've Got You Under My Skin • My One and Only Love • Satin Doll • Take the "A" Train • The Way You Look Tonight • and more.
00311557 ....$24.99

BIG BOOK OF LATIN AMERICAN SONGS

89 songs: Always in My Heart • Feelings (Dime?) • The Girl from Ipanema • Granada • It's Impossible • La Cucaracha • Malaguena • Manha de Carnaval (A Day in the Life of a Fool) • What a Diff'rence a Day Made • and more!
00311562 ....$22.99

BIG BOOK OF LOVE SONGS

82 songs: All of Me • Endless Love • (Everything I Do) I Do It for You • Just the Way You Are • My Heart Will Go On (Love Theme from 'Titanic') • The Power of Love • Thinking Out Loud • Unchained Melody • Wonderful Tonight • You Raise Me Up • and more.
00257807 ....$22.99

BIG BOOK OF MOTOWN

84 songs: Baby Love • Get Ready • I Heard It Through the Grapevine • Just My Imagination • Lady Marmalade • My Girl • Reach Out, I'll Be There • Shop Around • Three Times a Lady • You Are the Sunshine of My Life • and more.
00311061 ....$22.99

BIG BOOK OF MOVIE MUSIC

74 songs: Beauty and the Beast • City of Stars • Eye of the Tiger • How Far I'll Go • Theme from "Jaws" • Over the Rainbow • Singin' in the Rain • Skyfall • The Sound of Music • What a Wonderful World • and more.
00260523 ....$22.99

BIG BOOK OF NOSTALGIA

158 songs: After the Ball • The Bells of St. Mary's • The Darktown Strutters' Ball • A Good Man Is Hard to Find • I'm Always Chasing Rainbows • If I Had My Way • Oh! You Beautiful Doll • Pretty Baby • Swanee • You Made Me Love You (I Didn't Want to Do It) • and more.
00310004 ....$27.50

BIG BOOK OF OLDIES

73 songs: All My Loving • Barbara Ann • Crying • (Sittin' on) The Dock of the Bay • Good Vibrations • Great Balls of Fire • Kansas City • La Bamba • Mellow Yellow • Respect • Soul Man • Twist and Shout • Windy • and more.
00310756 ....$22.99

BIG BOOK OF STANDARDS

86 songs: April In Paris • Beyond the Sea • Blue Skies • Cheek to Cheek • I Left My Heart In San Francisco • Isn't It Romantic? • It's Impossible • Ol' Man River • Out Of Nowhere • Puttin' on the Ritz • Star Dust • That Old Black Magic • The Way We Were • What Now My Love • and more.
00311667 ....$19.95

BIG BOOK OF SWING

84 songs: Air Mail Special • Boogie Woogie Bugle Boy • In the Mood • Jukebox Saturday Night • Mood Indigo • Stompin' at the Savoy • A String of Pearls • Take the "A" Train • That Old Black Magic • Tuxedo Junction • and more.
00310359 ....$24.99

BIG BOOK OF TORCH SONGS

75 songs: All Alone • Bewitched • Crazy • Good Morning Heartache • Here's That Rainy Day • In a Sentimental Mood • Misty • 'Round Midnight • Stormy Weather • Too Young • and more.
00310561 ....$29.99

BIG BOOK OF TV THEME SONGS

71 songs: The Big Bang Theory • Breaking Bad • Downton Abbey • Friends • Game of Thrones • I Love Lucy • Jeopardy • M*A*S*H • NFL on Fox • The Office • The Simpsons • The Sopranos • Star Trek® • and more.
00294317 ....$24.99

BIG BOOK OF WEDDING MUSIC

77 songs: Ave Maria • Canon in D • Endless Love • In My Life • Jesu, Joy of Man's Desiring • The Lord's Prayer • Trumpet Voluntary • We've Only Just Begun • Wedding March • Wedding Processional • You Are So Beautiful • and more.
00311567 ....$22.99

HAL•LEONARD®